CW01034810

MAGIC in ACTION

MAGIC in ACTION

by
Richard Bandler

Meta Publications
P.O. Box 1910
Capitola, CA 95010
(831) 464-0254
Fax (831) 464-0517
www.meta-publications.com
email: metapub@prodigy.net

Library of Congress Card Number 84-061646
ISBN 10: 0-916990-14-1
ISBN 13: 978-0-916990-14-5

Contents

Publisher's Note

The following introduction has been excerpted from an interview with Richard Bandler in August 1990.

Introduction

At the time these sessions were recorded, the idea of curing a phobia in one session was as preposterous [as trying to fly to the moon]. Even people who said they could do that in ten one-hour sessions—they called that brief therapy back then—were being attacked. But at least those people had the attitude that if you can't cure a phobia in ten sessions you're probably not going to do it at all. So [at that time] this was considered really radical.

These client sessions happened because the people at Marshall University wanted to document one of these "loudmouths" who went around saying therapy is simple. Someone had made a film of Fritz Perls, Albert Ellis and Carl Rogers each seeing the same client. Afterwards they asked the client which of the three she like best and which one she thought would help her. But none of them really accomplished much in one session.

I was going around saying that you could actually fix a client quickly. I was always amazed that people needed to be convinced of this, especially professionals. Because if you can't do it in one session, what are you going to do in the next one?

If you could do one long session where you try everything you know and then make a list of all the other things you haven't tried yet it might help, but what's the point of using something that doesn't work over and over again? Some studies show that if you leave a client on a waiting list for ten years he gets better, and at least you're not charging him.

So the people at Marshall seemed to have a great opportunity to disprove me. I went in and saw the clients cold, in a studio, without even meeting them before we walked in. As I was arriving, one of the guys from Marshall came up to me and said, "By the way, Richard, it's the weekend, we could only get half-hour tapes. Is that going to be a problem?" "Yeah," I said. "What are your going to do with the rest of the tape?"

People who are so impressed by the speed of changes fail to understand that change not only *can* occur quickly, but it must occur quickly if you work with the natural processes by which clients create and sustain their problems, rather than with the content of those problems. As soon as you get involved in the content, you're ignoring the fact that everybody processes information differently, so you're actually selling ideology not doing change work. That's what most psychotherapies, or psychotheologies as Gregory Bateson called them, have been doing, and that's why they haven't worked–lots of theory, little skill. Those theories were derived from the medical model, which presupposed that something was wrong with people, so its followers treated people as if they had an infection or a broken leg. "You broke your leg when you were a kid, and it hurts you as an adult because it wasn't set right. Now we're going to go back and reset it so you can get better."

That's why patients have been focused on their pasts for decades. But if the past has made them the way they are now, focusing on it will only make them how they are now even more. The focus on the past and on a problem's content is the very reason clients are unable to overcome their problems after years of therapy. That model doesn't work the way the brain does.

The brain is an archival system, not a rewrite system. It doesn't have an erase function, so you don't get to rewrite your past. What you have to do is teach the brain to go in a new direction—"here" instead of "there."

It's like when you have moved but still drive to the old house until you build something in the brain that resets the automatic pilot ahead of time. The trick is to go back before the problem started and build a new pathway in your brain's "wiring" so you can forget about the problem. That doesn't mean, as people often believe, that you're covering up problems that will pop up somewhere else. You're not covering up problems, you're going around them in a more useful direction. You have to focus your attention in one direction and not another, so all you do is learn a better direction in which to focus your attention.

Magic in Action shows the ways in which I use humor and speed to work with clients. It gives the layman an idea of what an NLP session should be like. I constantly joke with clients about their problems in order to cure them of seriousness, which is what locks the model down. You get serious, you get stuck. Humor is the fastest way to reverse this process. As soon as you can laugh about something, you can change it.

And change doesn't need to be slow or painful. If you can learn to create something as sophisticated as a phobia, fear or compulsion, you can learn to use the same ability to do something different in the same situations.

If you're a layperson you shouldn't try to learn how to do these things from the book; you should learn what's possible. I want your unconscious to grasp that, just as the people in the transcripts changed the direction of their lives within a matter of moments, any of your problems can dissolve and you can begin to focus on your future possibilities just as quickly. Because no matter what your past was like, you always have a new future.

Instead of arguing with your spouse, doing the same boring things and having the same boring problems, as if they were conditioned responses, start to put a "no-whining" sign up in your life and say, "Enough is enough. I want this to be different."

If you have hope and tenacity you can get anything done. If you have what I have, impatience, you can forget about it and go on.

For the student of NLP *Magic in Action* is best used as a workbook. I recommend that you first read it through, then study the last transcript with the notation, and then go through and analyze all the transcripts. Underline the first four lines of whatever the client says at the beginning of each transcript, because often that's where the answer already is.

Also try other ways of chunking than the ones that are provided in the annotation. If you [look at it as] submodalities, what would happen? If you [look at it as] metamodel, what would happen? If you [think about it as] strategies, what would happen? If you [think about it as] metaprograms, what would happen? And one last problem: How does it all fit together? How did I know what to do? Because you don't know how the meta-model and the Milton-model, submodalities and representational systems, strategies and neurocortical pathways interact until you can put them all together at the same time in a model of the world.

Of course, the difference between a book and real-life experience cannot be overestimated. Books are sequential, life interactions are not. But part of developing expertise is breaking complex processes into pieces; if you can become skilled at that, you'll learn? achieve? that much more when you [go for] life performances of videotapes. Remember, though, to put the pieces back together into one whole. You don't just use the metamodel or timelines; you're using them all as detection tools, not as diagnostic tools. They tell you where to intervene to help people process information in a way that is more useful.

The techniques used in the client sessions and demonstrations, like the swish pattern or the phobia cure, are by now archaeology. These techniques are not what constitutes NLP. There are many solutions in every situation; if the only way you can get results is by a formatted fix, you are not a Neuro-Linguistic Programmer, you are a therapist with some NLP techniques.

What's most important of all is the attitude. Without the right attitude and belief systems you are just mouthing words, not doing NLP.

This attitude is easy to describe: anything is possible to accomplish. When you have that belief, you are able to suspend your present beliefs about what is possible and you can begin to find out what can be done. So no matter what difficulty you face, you will have two options: either you can do it or you can't do it yet, so you'll start looking for what you need to make it possible.

As soon as you assume that something can be done, you will always give it your best shot and find the tools and skills necessary to make it happen.

From an evolutionary perspective we have just crawled out of the swamp. We are only now beginning to find out what the human mind can do. Our cognitive evolution has just started. From now on that evolution can be more conscious and deliberate.

People in the change business talk about therapy, problem-solving and mental health like they're the end. but in fact we haven't even begun to find out how good we can feel! Once we understand this, we can begin to ask ourselves, "Well, if I can turn the anxieties down, what else can I turn up? How about something I haven't had yet? Can I make up new feelings?"

The challenge of NLP is to enable people to take control of their cognitive evolution and to realize that their internal pictures, voices and feelings belong to them and that they can manipulate them the same way they use their fingers to turn a doorknob.

The challenge is to help people understand that what they thought was reality is just their own model of reality, and to move them to a position where they can say, "If that's just a model, I'd rather have that one over there."

As soon as you can make it that simple, without the crying and the sniveling and all the personal history, you are good at what you're doing. But in order to make it that simple you must have complex skills.

I want everybody who is interested in NLP to know that this is serious work, although it doesn't mean you have to act seriously while you're doing it. There is a lot to learn about syntax, voice tone, eye movements, metaprograms and all those things, but I can say beyond a doubt that I took what I learned from Virginia Satir, Milton Erickson, Bill Feldman, and all for the great communicators and went further than they ever could have dreamed of because I learned form them.

If you want to compliment somebody, go further than they went.

This introduction is from a conversation between Richard Bandler and the editor.

Chapter One

Anticipatory Loss

The client in this session, Susan, experiences acute anxiety whenever somebody is late.

This case is a good example of something you will encounter when you work with NLP: the clinical terminology often obscures what is really going on. I have found very little correlation in the change business between the ability to create nominalizations or diagnostic systematizations and the ability to create change. It's the opposite—the ability to denominalize—that creates skill.

In this case Susan creates her anxiety in much the same way people create stage fright, fear of public speaking, fear of flying, etc. She has a fear, not a phobia. Clinicians often get them mixed up, but they're very different animals.

People frequently come for the treatment of phobias, such as flying phobias, who do not really have a flying phobia. When they are on the plane, they're fine. Their anxiety precedes the actual event. It is created by a mental procedure of shifting and manipulating internal states. Phobias are the outcome of a stimulus-response event.

Both fear and phobias are easily treatable; they just have to be treated differently. If it's a fear you change the part of the process that creates the fear. It's common with stage fright, for example, for people to make pictures of audiences in their heads that would scare me, too. In that case you simply change the picture to something else—a happy audience, for example. It makes more sense for the person to think about what he wants to do on stage than to see himself getting lynched by creatures with gigantic heads and unblinking eyes.

If it's a phobia, you dilute the intensity of the feeling to a level where you can switch to a more useful feeling.

Neither anxieties nor phobias are disorders. They show how easily and pervasively human beings learn.

Notice how, within the thirty minutes of this session, Susan's attitude changes. She goes from believing that something was wrong with her to seeing her panic attacks as something she had learned to do. Finally, not without a sense of pride, she realizes she is an expert at a skill she could teach me.

Her ability to generate panic attacks, and to understand how she is doing it with her own mind, is the same ability, used in a new way, that allows her to overcome this difficulty.

Students of NLP should notice that the session doesn't actually portray a phobia cure. In fact, Susan's first answer basically reveals what she needs to overcome her fear:

Richard   Okay Susan. Now why don't you tell me what it is that you would like? I don't know. We just got brought here and wired up, so you have to give me a hint.

Susan   Okay. I have a problem with a fear that is almost disabling to me at certain times. When I have it I sort of go into panic attacks. What I would like to do is distance myself . . .

In Susan's case the distance of images is the critical variable for a lasting change that gives her control over the quality of her life.

———————

Bill   This is one of a series of video tapes featuring Richard Bandler, the originator and co-founder of Neuro-Linguistic Programming. Sitting here with me is Michael Saggese, who's going to help in narrating these films today. Michael, we certainly have been very fortunate in having Dr. Bandler in this series, and I think a unique experience because though Dr. Bandler appears on a number of video tapes it's usually with an audience and that kind of thing and these are studio quality tapes. It certainly gives us a different preview of him, working with one individual in that particular setting.

Michael   I want to comment on that a moment Bill, the fact that it is a studio quality tape. The fact that we've gone to great efforts to emphasize the quality, as well as the fact that these are some of the first tapes you'll ever see with follow-up. We've gone . . . the fact when this tape is over you'll see an eight-month follow-up with the individual that

	Richard has worked with. I think it adds a uniqueness to this tape.
Bill	It certainly does. I think it helps people see that this is not something that was temporary, but something that had a long lasting value.
Michael	Right.
Bill	A lot of the people who are watching this video tape may never have heard of Neuro-Linguistic Programming, and that's a mouthful, before. If you were having to tell someone very briefly what NLP was, how would you describe it to them?
Michael	That's a good question. What I would like to do is emphasize what NLP, for me, the most important things. NLP in one sense is a way of modeling other behavior. But unique in the sense that it allows one to begin to understand the structure of internal experience. What I mean by that is that our experiences are made up of visualization, auditory experiences and feelings and NLP is the first model that I know of that has been able to look at the relationship between how we neuro-logically process information, and its effect on our behavior and feelings.
Bill	So the emphasis being on internal experience as opposed to just looking at external experience.
Michael	Well the emphasis on how our internal experience or how we process information affects our external experience and our interaction with

other people. Specifically as you watch Richard work with Susan in this tape, he begins to explore, if you will, her internal experiences, her visual images. How she sees herself in the situations that bring on these uncomfortable feelings as well as how she visualizes the experience.

Bill   He does do a great deal of work with her visualization patterns.

Michael   Yes he does.

Bill   And they seem different than just saying, do you see something? He does a lot of changing of patterns.

Michael   There's a word in NLP we call submodalities. And what that word means is you take a visual field or take a picture; there are a number of ways you can adjust the picture. You can make it bright, you can make it dark. You can increase its size.

Bill   Sort of like you work a television set.

Michael   Precisely. It's like having fine tuning. You can adjust the clarity of the picture. You can adjust the distance of the picture. And as you will notice as Dr. Bandler begins to ask her questions to elicit information you'll notice her feeling and her experience begins to change as he adjusts that internal image. NLP is the only model that I know that gives you that technology to begin to

understand and give you the tool with which to
begin to alter internal experience so rapidly.

Bill   So it would be very helpful I think for those
            viewing the tape to look at the manual because
            the manual would be more explicit on the sub-
            modalities as you call them, so that one might be
            able to look at the tape and know not only what
            to look for but how to find it.

Michael   Precisely.

Bill   So that would be a valuable asset for them. As
            people look at this tape there's certainly a lot of
            things in the manual that they could look at and
            utilize, but would there be any other thing that
            you would particularly want people to be sure as
            they're viewing this, that they ought to be aware
            of?

Michael   I would suggest that people listen for and look for
            two things specifically as they watch Dr. Bandler
            work. One is to notice Susan's eye accessing
            movements and her behavior as she tries to get or
            elicit the information that Dr. Bandler asks for.
            But also begin to look at how he systematically
            elicits information from her to find out what it is
            that creates the unpleasant experience. It's almost
            like Richard is one to talk about the difference
            that makes a difference. And what is the difference
            in the situation that for Susan allows her to not
            get so upset about the experience.

Bill	Once he understands that he begins to change what that pattern is. How she goes about that.
Michael	That's right. And once he begins to change that internal pattern experience, the external behavior is subsequently going to be changed. We will hopefully see that in the follow up that we do at the end of the tape.
Bill	And now we'll turn to Dr. Richard Bandler as he works with Susan.
Richard	Okay Susan. Now why don't you tell me what it is that you would like? I don't know. We just got brought here and wired up, so you have to give me a hint.
Susan	Okay. I have a problem with a fear that is almost disabling to me at certain times. When I have it I sort of go into panic attacks. What I would like to do is distance myself so that when I'm in the situation that I wouldn't experience the fear to the degree that I have it. Where I could control myself and make better decisions.
Richard	Is the fear appropriate? It's not like you're afraid of death lying in bed or something like that.
Susan	No, it's a fear of loss. It's a fear of losing friendships or close relationships. Even when I anticipate a loss that isn't even real I get a panic attack.
Richard	The situation that you are worried about being in is the one of anticipating and thinking about the loss?

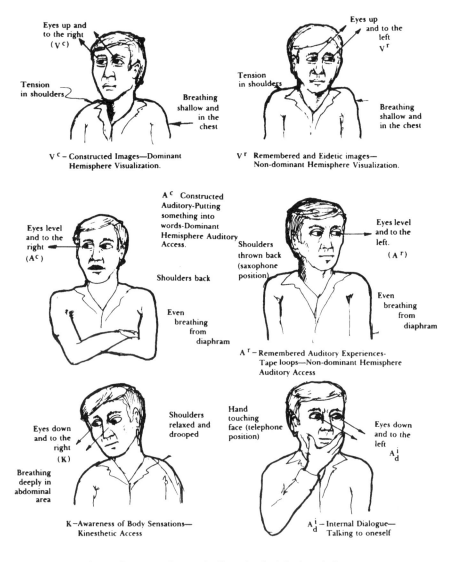

Eyes up and to the right (V^c)

Tension in shoulders

Breathing shallow and in the chest

V^c – Constructed Images—Dominant Hemisphere Visualization.

Eyes up and to the left V^r

Tension in shoulders

Breathing shallow and in the chest

V^r Remembered and Eidetic images—Non-dominant Hemisphere Visualization.

A^c Constructed Auditory-Putting something into words-Dominant Hemisphere Auditory Access.

Eyes level and to the right (A^c)

Shoulders back

Even breathing from diaphram

Shoulders thrown back (saxophone position)

Eyes level and to the left. (A^r)

Even breathing from diaphram

A^r – Remembered Auditory Experiences-Tape loops—Non-dominant Hemisphere Auditory Access

Eyes down and to the right (K)

Breathing deeply in abdominal area

Shoulders relaxed and drooped

K –Awareness of Body Sensations—Kinesthetic Access

Hand touching face (telephone position)

Eyes down and to the left A_d^i

A_d^i – Internal Dialogue—Talking to oneself

Accessing cues for typically wired right-handed person.

Susan   Right. I guess, yes.

Richard   Do you lose a lot of friends?

Susan	No.
Richard	I was going to say, maybe I wouldn't hang around with you too much.
Susan	No, I really don't.
Richard	When you first said loss I grabbed for my wallet here.
Susan	No, it relates though to people and not possessions.
Richard	So it's mostly about animate things?
Susan	Yes.
Richard	Let me ask you a question. If I was going . . . let's say I had to fill in for you. How do you know when to have the fear? How do you do this? Can you do it now?
Susan	Yes. If someone . . . well I can in a way. For instance, if you told me that you were going to be here to meet me for this session and we were close friends so that it mattered to me, and then you were late . . .
Richard	It's been known to happen.
Susan	Then I might think that you weren't coming at all, and I would begin to get a panic attack.
Richard	Oh. With certain people it could be something that goes on on a frequent basis?

Susan   Right.

Richard   There are them that are always late. But how do
               you do it? How do you know, how do you get
               the panic?

Susan   Do you mean what feelings do I get?

Richard   Let's say I had to fill in for you for a day. So one
               of the parts of my job would be if somebody was
               late I'd have to have the panic for you. What do I
               do inside my head in order to have the panic?[1]

---

1. Underneath this description is a message to the client that she is doing something in
her mind to produce the undesired result. And if somebody says, "You can teach me to
do this," it presupposes that she can stop doing it.
     The point is to find any means to alter how your interaction with a client is struc-
tured so you can switch the desired behavior from impossible to possible.
     By saying I'm from a temporary agency, it also puts the client in control. It makes
her, not me, the one who knows, so it reduces the attitude that "you have to be an
expert to understand." This approach can also cure therapists of overwhelming
pompousness, as it presupposes the whole interaction is centered around the client having the answer, not me.
     That's what changes attitudes. It also, even in this example, highlights the differ-
ence between truth, reality and a model. In other words, it's not the truth that she has a
problem and it's not reality, because now she's telling me what her model is, so that I
can [do it.]
     Therapists often make the mistake of saying, "Other people have had this problem
and they were able to stop it." Immediately she will see herself as different: "Well, I'm
not like other people. My phobia is different. My problem is different." But if you say,
"Look, you have to teach me to be the way you are," it changes the whole frame.
Instead of confronting the issue cognitively, you're having her act "as if."
     You can't convince people that what they're living is not the truth. They are
trapped in it because it feels real to them. And as long as it feels real, it doesn't feel like
it's just their model of the world that is the problem. It only makes them feel more
helpless.
     What you want to do is put people in a position of power, not helplessness.
Helplessness prevents people from even looking at the edge of their model. By putting
clients in a powerful position, you give them what it takes to make the changes they
need.

Susan	You start telling yourself sentences like . . .
Richard	I've got to talk to myself.
Susan	Hmm, so and so is late, look they're not here. That means that they may never come.
Richard	Do I say this in a casual tone of voice?
Susan	No . . .
Richard	They're late . . . I think I'll panic now.
Susan	No, you start out slowly, because you start saying, they still have time. I'll give them another half an hour and if they're not here by then . . .
Richard	I'll panic. That gives me half an hour to change the speed of the internal dialogue.
Susan	But as the time goes on it begins to build.
Richard	How do I know what to talk about . . . do you make any pictures in there too?
Susan	Yes. Pictures of whoever it is that isn't there. Maybe pictures of them . . .
Richard	Pictures of whoever it is that isn't there.
Susan	The person who should be coming and hasn't come.
Richard	What kind of pictures?
Susan	Pictures of their face.

Richard   From the past, will you make up new ones?

Susan   Ones of just what they look like, or maybe
              pictures of them in a wreck.

Richard   Pictures of them in a wreck?

Susan   Yes.

Richard   Okay, when you see them in a wreck . . . From
              what point of view? Do you see it like from the
              side? Do you see it like out of their eyes? What do
              you do?

Susan   No. I see it as if I were standing looking on.

Richard   From what? From the side?

Susan   I guess it's from the side. I really hadn't thought
              about it. I think it's from the side.

Richard   So first I do it, is it a panoramic thing? Do you
              have borders on your screen?

Susan   No it's just more like a zoom in I guess.

Richard   A zoom in. There are no edges on your pictures
              then?

Susan   No.

Richard   Do you actually move closer to it? When you
              make the pictures then?

Susan   I'm trying to think . . . Yes I do.

Richard	This is a timed test you know. You actually zoom in. How close do you get? Do you get right up to their face? Do you do that with the wreck?
Susan	Probably only as close to them as I would be like if they were injured and I was someone treating them or helping them.
Richard	That's pretty close. When you started out you said you wanted to get some distance from this problem. Can you stop now and remember a time when you, the last time, had one of these panic things and remember what pictures you make?
Susan	Yes. I had one last night. That time I made some pictures of a wreck, but actually I just made pictures of the person, probably about as close to me as you are.
Richard	What did you say you do for a living?
Susan	I'm a nurse.
Richard	Oh, you're a nurse. Do you work in emergency wards?
Susan	I do some emergency work but actually I work in psychiatry. I handle psychiatric emergencies.
Richard	Okay. Now it makes more sense to me. I have another question too. If you don't see them in a wreck then where do you get the panic from?
Susan	Well the other thing that I see besides the person who isn't there is I see myself alone and lonely.

Richard	From what position?
Susan	In that case I'm looking through my own eyes out at the world.
Richard	You're looking through your own eyes out at the world. So you're not seeing yourself.
Susan	Occasionally I guess I see myself standing there sort of all alone in my house. But at other times it's just the lonely me and more like feelings. Sort of looking out at the world.
Richard	Do you see the planet down there?
Susan	No, no, no. Just as you would if you were like standing in your yard or something.
Richard	But there's nobody there.
Susan	Right.
Richard	I'll tell you what. Let's try a little experiment. Okay?
Susan	Okay.
Richard	Do you like to play?
Susan	Sure.
Richard	You remember what you did last night. At what point do you begin to feel the panic?
Susan	When I think that the person is later than is reasonable. A lot of times I can say, well I need to

cut them some slack and allow some distance. I mean, allow them some time. Then I start thinking they'll never come, they'll never come.[2]

Richard   Oh, that's good. That ought to work.

Susan   And then I really get worked up.

Richard   Then if you say they'll never come, then of course you have to make pictures to justify how they wouldn't get there. Like a wreck or something.

Susan   Yes, a wreck or even just to see them go into their own home or something like that and not keeping their appointment or whatever with me.

Richard   And you panic?

Susan   Um huh.

Richard   If you were to have distance how would you know you had it?

Susan   Well I believe I wouldn't feel those feelings. I'd have confidence, some self-confidence and I think I could say to myself, well, just because they're not here now doesn't mean that you've lost them and it really doesn't matter. Maybe something happened. And also you can go on. So what if they don't show up? You can go on.

Richard   You've obviously mastered this. By the way, do you know that this is an accomplishment?[2]

Susan   You mean to master the panic?

Richard   I bet you a lot of people here couldn't panic.

Susan   Probably not. Not like I do I'm sure.

Richard   It's like everything else. It's learned. Don't twiddle your microphone there or people back there are going to start yelling at us. There's a real difference between my view of people which is that one of the things about people is that they are such exquisite learners. I'm always amazed at how people can learn things so quickly. A lot of what they learn is not worth having learned. Think about how many futile things you've learned. But the fact that you can learn all those things is really impressive. For example, can you stop now and remember the same pictures that you were remembering last night? And get back the feeling of panic?

Susan   Yes. Pretty much.

Richard   Take the picture and literally zoom closer.

Susan   Okay. I'll close my eyes and do this. Shut out the light.

Richard   Everybody in the room leaves too, when you shut your eyes?

---

2. Since this was an unconscious mental process, it never occurred to Susan that she was deliberately acting that way. Slowing the process down enough helps people realize what they are doing. She recognized that her behavior was not something out of her control, not some psychiatric disorder that needed to be diagnosed; this was something she was actively doing, just like washing dishes or something else.

Susan	Right.
Richard	It's the Ostrich complex. That works doesn't it?
Susan	Yes.
Richard	The rest of the people here, they can't do that. You can actually stop and by literally zooming in on that picture . . . it's like a zoom lens, isn't it? As you zoom in on that picture you panic?
Susan	Right.
Richard	Go back to the picture real close and try un-zooming it. Even further. And further, further. Even more. How does that change your experience?
Susan	I don't feel as panicky.
Richard	Let me show you something else. Go back and look at it again from a distance. Now make the picture darker. Have you ever seen the brightness knob on the television? Turn the brightness down. What happens?
Susan	It creates more distance. Makes it fade away.
Richard	Makes it fade away. Turn the brightness up. Make it brighter. You do this real good. You're fast. And brighter. Now make it closer. What happens now as you make it closer and brighter at the same time?
Susan	I start getting feelings of tension and anxiety.

Richard   It works. Now the only difference is, is this time
                 you did it deliberately. See, I have this saying that
                 I tell people. Your brain is an amazing device in
                 the way that it works. The ability that people
                 have to learn is phenomenal. The thing about
                 people's brains is they're going to learn and do
                 things whether or not you're doing it. Most
                 people don't act with volition. They kind of act
                 like their brain is not something that they can use.
                 Your hands move whether you think about them
                 or not. If you stop, say you accidentally sat back
                 and placed your hand somewhere that was little
                 bit too warm you would go OHHHHHH and
                 pull it away. You can even voluntarily take it and
                 put it close. But if it starts to get warm you have
                 the choice of pulling back. That means you can
                 run your hand. Some people better than others. I
                 have a friend who comes over and breaks my
                 glasses constantly. Not these kind of glasses but
                 the ones on the table. You pour him a glass of
                 wine he reaches for it and his hand inevitably
                 knocks it over. He has not learned to run his hand
                 yet. But yet, he won't say that he doesn't have the
                 choice of steering it. With people's brains I always
                 ask them the question, Who's driving the bus in
                 there? If you don't run your brain they get mad at
                 you and go, Let's scare the hell out of her. If
                 you're capable of reliving the past unpleasantness,
                 you have a photographic memory. You could use
                 that, for example, imagine if you could see pages
                 of books and focus in that closely you could read
                 them again. Have a whole library there. What you
                 use to create panic is what I use to remember

check stubs and things like that. It's a lot more fun to remember them depending upon whether or not there's money in my checking account. Let me have you try something which is that what I'd like you to do is going to sound a little bit strange. But then most of the things I ask people to do are strange. When you see yourself being alone, for example, I'd like you to try, because we're going to do two things here. What I want you to do is to first make a picture of how you think you would be if you were able to change this. See it's not enough. I'm known as the greedy agent of change. It's not enough to solve problems for me because I don't believe in what you talk about as difficulty. I'm amazed at it. It works perfectly. You can go back and move right in and have panic. You can take the picture and move it. For example, go ahead and make the picture bright and focus in on it. Close your eyes again, move right in and as you approach very closely to it you begin to feel the panic. What I want you to do is to see in the small, lower left hand corner a little tiny dark square that has a picture of you the way you would be if you had made this change. It's real darkened in the corner but suddenly the big picture begins to get darker and the other one begins to expand and become brighter until it fills the whole screen. But you can do it faster than that. There you go. Hurry up. Until you can see yourself the way you would be. Now I want you to do the exact same thing. I want you to do it five times real fast. But I don't want you to shrink the big picture down. I want you to do blanks.

	You've got blanks in there? Is your blank black or white? I'm taking a survey.
Susan	I guess different days it's different. White today, I guess.
Richard	Alright. It's good we're in the south here. Five times. So you go whooosh. Do it once. Do it again. One, two, three, that was five. Lost count there, huh?
Susan	Yes.
Richard	What I'd like you to do is go back and do it three times. Only this time I want you to do it real fast. Just whooosh. Don't take any longer than that. That's the amount I want you to take. Do it three times? Okay. Do you like the feeling you get when you see yourself? Confident in the way you would be if you made this change?
Susan	Yes.
Richard	You like that feeling?
Susan	Very much.
Richard	What I want you to do is to go back to the memory of last night and remember the panic. In other words, go back and do the thing that would build the panic. Can you stay in the panic? Now put the little square in the corner and this time as the square expands the other square, the

larger one, I want you to have it move backwards as it fades. Then I want the other one to come closer as it expands.

So to speak, you'll end up face to face with yourself in a new situation.

How does that feel as you get there?

Susan	It feels a lot better.
Richard	I want you to do that three times very rapidly.
Susan	Okay.
Richard	As I told you there are two things that we had to do. This is number two.
	Oh come on, you can do it faster.
Susan	I'm finished now.
Richard	Okay, once again, I want you to go back and go back to the image from which the panic was. As you get closer, this time I want you to turn it so bright it turns white.
	And then make it dark. And as you make it darker in the lower left hand corner the other image will expand and get brighter as it expands till it fills the full screen.
	I told you this wasn't going to be hard. You have pretty good pictures in there. You're a little slow with them. See, I like high-speed movies. Do it again once, but do it faster, alright?
Susan	Um huh.

Richard   You go ahead this time and go back and look at
             that panic. See if you can hold it. I want you to
             try as much as you can in vain.

Susan   It's hard. I just keep getting white.

Richard   What do you mean?

Susan   I'm having trouble doing it.

Richard   I thought you'd mastered panic.

Susan   I am a master at panic. Right now all I'm getting
             is white.

Richard   Well, pick a different time. You must have pan-
             icked more than once.

             You may have lost your skill.

Susan   I can get the panic but it's not as intense.

Richard   Go ahead and try and keep the not as intense
             panic.

Susan   It just isn't working. (Laughter)

Richard   Uh oh. You got tricked. You see, it's not so hard
             to change, is it?

Susan   Not really.

Richard   Try it once more. Just to be sure.

Susan   I really just can't do it.

Richard	With utter confidence. You've got to keep your promise. You said it would change your whole life.
Susan	Yeah.
Richard	Now you have to keep your end of the bargain.
Susan	Well I think if I don't have this problem that it is going to change. Because it's going to affect everything.
Richard	You got a new one. You're not going to be able to do it.
Susan	That would be wonderful.
Richard	Try it.
Susan	I've tried it.
Richard	Try it right now.
Susan	I just can't get it. I just can't get it.
Richard	Well if it was so easy before and it's so hard now, that's an indication. You can go try it in the real world. I tell you what. Why don't you go outside by the coffee machine and I'll meet you there in ten minutes?
Susan	Okay.
Richard	Okay. Thank you.

Bill   It's been some eight months since Dr. Richard
            Bandler worked with Susan and a problem that
            she described as suffering from some anticipatory
            loss. Susan, we're glad after this period of time to
            have you back and give us this opportunity to find
            out, to follow up just kind of what's happened
            that you remember from that day and what's been
            your experience since then.

            We had some questions we wanted to ask her,
            because we've really been anticipating this kind of
            follow up that we are uniquely able to offer for
            people.

Michael   I guess what I'd like to start off with Susan, is as
            you think back on the time you spent with Dr.
            Bandler, what, for you, seemed to be the most
            helpful, was the most important thing that he did?

Susan   I'm trying to remember. It's a little difficult for
            me in a way to pinpoint anything. But, I guess,
            the one thing that I do remember is whiting out
            the bad picture of me and also blowing up the
            vision of myself as I wanted to be. It's much easier
            for me now to visualize myself as I would like to
            be. That's really about all I remember from the
            session.

Michael   How specifically are you different now? Let's say
            you get into a situation where someone is maybe
            twenty minutes late to meet you for a luncheon
            or a meeting. How are you different?

Susan   It's really good. I don't panic when someone's
            late. I'm able to look at the situation, visualize

myself as I want to be and I don't panic. I can think of plenty of good reasons that they might be late and I'm able to just handle the situation sensibly.

Bill

How long did it take for that to start happening?

Susan

That's really interesting. When I left the studio that day I knew that I felt really good but I was still a little skeptical of what had happened because my panics are so bad and so painful to me. I went home that evening and the same situation occurred. Someone was supposed to come and they didn't show up for several hours. And I didn't get upset at all. I was able to lie down and take a nap. It didn't upset me at all. I was just truly amazed.

Michael

Like Bill mentioned, we're eight months down the road now from the original time you spent with Richard. How are you still doing? Are you still finding that you don't get as upset as you used to?

Susan

I don't get nearly as upset. Sometimes when I'm faced with a real loss I do get upset. But it's more of an appropriate upsetness. For example, my best friend moved to Texas in November. I shed tears when she left but I didn't panic. So it was an appropriate type of response to a real loss.

Michael

Let me see if I understand something for the purpose of the tape. I believe I hear you saying that two things at least have changed. One is in a situation where someone may, is supposed to meet you and they may be several hours late, your internal image of yourself is different. And so is your internal image of the situation.

Susan   Yes.

Michael   So that you do not begin to have these panicky feelings.

Susan   Right.

Michael   And that change is still holding up more than eight months down the road now.

Susan   Right.

Michael   How do you feel about that?

Susan   You don't know what a relief it is!

Michael   That's very nice to hear. Very pleased to hear that.

Bill   You know one of the things that is amazing I think as we watch about twenty minutes or so that Dr. Bandler worked with you is that many people would be very excited to do this kind of work. But we really want to caution our viewers of the video tape in that to do the kinds of things that Dr. Bandler is doing can be learned, but they should be learned under a supervision of a trainer of Neuro-Linguistic Programming and with people who have the credentials to do that kind of training. We're going to, at the end of the tape, show you some of those different resources that are available in learning NLP and we certainly, again, want you to look at the manual for some more specifics about the training in Neuro-Linguistic Programming. Michael, do you have a closing thought yourself?

Michael   The only caution I would add in closing the tape is when you watch Richard work he makes it look so simple. What he's actually doing is very sophisticated and I think it's important that people enjoy the tapes, use them as learning tools but be sure to spend some time with someone who is certified as a trainer in Neuro-Linguistic Programming before they begin experimenting on themselves or other people.

Bill   Susan, thank you very much for being with us.

Susan   Thank you.

Conclusion

For readers who are not NLP students but interested observers, notice how the manipulation of internal states, such as the size of images, the position of images and the volume of internal voices, offers a wealth of possibilities for controlling your brain. If you would like a further understanding of these processes, see *Using Your Brain for a Change* (Real People Press, 1985).

The student of NLP will notice that although the session with Susan was very short, it was lasting and powerful. The importance of distance as the critical parameter is demonstrated in two ways—first, by using the swish pattern with the parameter of size, which didn't prove pervasive enough for Susan to maintain. Then, in repeating the process and adding distance as a parameter, I achieved a lasting effect.

Students of NLP should keep in mind that it always takes two analog and one digital submodality for the swish pattern to produce lasting change.

Chapter 2

Agoraphobia

Although Lee is listed as agoraphobic, his case is not standard agoraphobia. Lee is able to leave his house; he is just not able to leave the town where he lives. The mere though of leaving town produces a response that is stronger than a panic attack (see previous chapter). This problem has become so crippling to Lee that he has attempted to leave town only a few times over a number of years.

Lee has received psychiatric treatment, and there is a host of different labels for his disorder. But his problem isn't a disorder to begin with. It is an example of Lee's learning ability. Whatever happened that led Lee to associate leaving Huntington, West Virginia, with terror—and those of you who have been to Huntington realize that it's a place that offers quite limited choices—it doesn't take more than a series of disassociations to reduce the impact of the semantic response to the neuro-synaptic charge, and therefore reduce the intensity of his feelings to where he can handle them, eliciting at the same time humor and excitement. These new feelings are then associated with the thought of leaving town. After fifteen minutes Lee is not only able to leave town but to drive out of the state.

Whenever feelings overwhelm an individual, the goal of NLP is first to reduce the intensity of the feelings and then to switch them to something more appropriate.

To think of every difficulty as a psychiatric problem, or to focus on things that went wrong in people's pasts negates their ability to learn positive and useful things as easily as totally foolish things. The rule for computers is "garbage in—garbage out," but humans are much the same way. Sixteen years of therapeutic "garbage in" did not produce any satisfying output, while fifteen minutes of NLP created an opportunity for Lee to use his ability to learn quickly and easily. He had no problem to overcome, just something new to learn. In that sense the session is not so much a phobia cure as it is a partial model that's really about learning.

———————

Bill   This is one of a series of video tape presentations featuring Dr. Richard Bandler, co-founder, originator and developer of Neuro-Linguistic Programming. With me today, serving as narrator is Michael Saggese. Michael, we've certainly been fortunate in having Dr. Bandler in this series, working with us and also working with three very important and, I must say, courageous clients to come before a camera to expose to some degree a problem that they have. Though in many cases we have found that Dr. Bandler can work with situations where we really don't need to know exactly what's happening. Perhaps that tells us something of the uniqueness of approach in Neuro-Linguistic Programming. In terms of how it deals with people. Could you speak to that?

Michael	I'd like to speak to a couple comments you made, Bill. The uniqueness of this whole situation strikes me as being very exciting. To have Dr. Bandler here in the studio. To work live with people. To have the opportunity to do follow up with them. To see how easy he makes it look as he works with people, working with very complicated human problems.
Bill	In fact that's probably one of the things that is dangerous to some degree. That people shouldn't see this tape and think, well anybody can do that. That they really should receive training in order to do this kind of thing.
Michael	I agree wholeheartedly. To go back into the other part of your question, although the gentleman we're going to see, the present tape is working with the phobia, in many ways the uniqueness of NLP, since it deals with the structure of an experience and specifically the structure of your internal experience. I don't necessarily need to know the content of the material. I don't have to spend a lot of time asking maybe embarrassing questions to the person about things that are difficult to talk about.
Bill	So you're really concentrating on the process as opposed to content.
Michael	Talking about process, talking about structure. To me one of the things that makes NLP extremely unique is being able to understand the structure of someone's internal experience. And by this

structure what I'm talking about are the images or visualizations. The sounds or auditory track, internal kinesthetic feelings that a person goes through which create their internal experiences and influence their external behavior.

Bill   How would that work in working with a person who has a phobia, as we're going to see Dr. Bandler doing in a moment?

Michael   One of the things that's unique in NLP for me is that it's the first model that ever gave me a real indication of what's happening with someone who's phobic. Someone who is phobic has had some experience at some point in time that they may or may not remember that, it's the greatest example of one-shot learning. If you've never seen someone who's phobic of elevators, get into an elevator and forget to be phobic. It's like they have that one experience and from then on whenever they get near whatever it is that creates that anxiety or that unpleasant feeling always creates an unpleasant feeling. The analogy I like to use is like a roller coaster. If you and I are sitting here watching a roller coaster go up the very first incline, we may be able to hear the sound of the wheels as they click over the tracks. We may hear the people getting excited. We may have feelings about that. But if you and I were to switch positions at the time that car reached the apex at the top of the first drop so that you and I were sitting in the front car holding onto the seats when the thing went down, those are two drastically different experiences.

Bill	Yes.
Michael	And what's happening with the phobic is they're always in the front seat. It's like if you have certain memories and think about them, there's some memories that you have . . . they're somewhat like watching a movie, you see yourself.
Bill	So Bandler wants to change how the perspective of Lee as . . .
Michael	In this experience. From being someone who's actively in an experience that's unpleasant, helping him to, what we call disassociate so that he can see the experience differently.
Bill	Well, one of the things about working with phobias is that often it took a very long time to help someone with a phobia. Maybe ten or eighteen sessions. One thing very unique about Neuro-Linguistic Programming is Dr. Bandler is going to work with a phobic person here and hopefully bring about change in about twenty minutes.
Michael	I think one of the things that allows him to do that is the fact that he understands the structure of the experience. You can take a particular discipline and you can try to find out when something started and how you feel about it and go through it. Or we can begin to understand the structure of that experience. And if I restructure it or alter it in some definite way I most assuredly am going to affect how I feel about that experience. And as I restructure or change your position from one of being in

an emotional experience that's overwhelming to being back and looking at something from a different perspective I'm surely going to change how you feel about yourself and the experience.

Bill   When people are looking at this video tape we want to tell them that there is a manual that accompanies the tape that can have a number of helps for you in what to look for and how to understand the experience that you are going to observe. But, Michael, as they're looking right now, what would you have them to look for?

Michael   I would have them look for and listen for a couple of things. One is to notice how Dr. Bandler gets to understand what specifically happens internally with Lee. How he creates this anxiety or this phobic response. And then to notice what specifically Dr. Bandler does to change the internal experience. The other thing I would caution people about, and as we've mentioned on the other tapes, is Dr. Bandler makes this work look awfully simple and awfully easy. And although it can be once you understand and learn the model I think you would agree with me that we highly recommend that in order to really use this model effectively one needs to spend time training with a certified trainer in Neuro-Linguistic Programming and make sure that you know what you're doing. It's a very powerful technique.

Bill   Yes it is. And now we'll see that powerful technique with Richard Bandler.

Richard   What's your name?

Lee   Lee.

Richard   Lee. That's your first name?

Lee   Right.

Richard   Correct. That's one right answer you've got so
            far. What is it that you'd like, Lee? You just sat
            and watched *her* go through that.

Lee   Well, . . . I have oh I guess you call it panic
            attacks.

Richard   What is it, is there something down here that's
            scaring the hell out of people? **What's going on
            here?**

Lee   A phobia or whatever you want to call it, a panic
            attack. I have trouble getting outside the city
            limits. When I do driving . . .

Richard   Outside of the city as opposed to coming in?

Lee   No, just staying in when I try to go is when I
            have most of them. Mostly.

Richard   Oh, that's different. I have panic when I go into
            the city. I think based on the real experience. Of
            course I go to cities like New York, San
            Francisco, that's enough to get anybody to panic.
            They have hills there you wouldn't believe.
            You've got to get used to the driving there. But I
            take it this is a little bit different. Does it happen

right at the city limits or do you kind of edge your way into it? Is there a sign that says, you are now leaving the city–panic!

Lee   No, I guess I just tell myself that when I get ready to go, it kind of starts on me a little bit.

Richard   Even before you leave the house?

Lee   Even if I think about it.

Richard   Even if you just think about it? When you think about it do you make pictures or talk to yourself about it?

Lee   When somebody mentions going somewhere, I'll start . . .

Richard   Don't be vague, we're under time pressure here.

Lee   When somebody says something about going outside the city limits, going somewhere my first thought is say no. I can't, I make excuses . . .

Richard   Does something happen in your head or that's just an involuntary response?

Lee   Well I guess now it's a response mostly. You know, I say I'll get these panic attacks and stuff and it bothers me so I just don't go.

Richard   Well if I were to suggest that after we left here, you and I drive out into the country, do you get panic when you think about that?

Lee   If I knew I had to do it, yeah.

Richard   Well you do. I test my work you know.

Lee   Oh really?

Richard   Yeah. This is the real world we're living in. The
           only thing you could possibly have more panic
           toward could be my wrath of you, as a client I
           want to test you. I've taken people kicking and
           screaming into elevators to test the phobia. When
           they got in there they discovered the only thing
           they had a phobia of then was me. They were fine.
           But I just want to know how you get to the panic,
           Can you do it now? Think about going . . . [1]

Lee   Not really. If I was in a car getting ready to . . .

Richard   Oh, well try it. Close your eyes and pretend that
           you see what you would see if you were getting
           into a car. And know what it looks like to drive
           out towards . . .

Lee   In the open spaces, yes.

---

1. When I tell him to think about driving, beads of sweat start forming on his skin. The
terror on his face is amazing. He can't think about it; the neurons connected with the
phenomenon of leaving town are highly charged. They are actually raised physically in
his brain, and they lead straight to terror. The technique I'm using doesn't make any
literal sense, but it does flatten out that charge.

   Disassociation is not a cognitive phenomenon; it's a physical event. Once you flatten out the charge you try to make something actually happen. The reason I run things
in reverse is that clients have never done it that way before. It creates a new pathway to
humor, because it looks like a Charlie Chaplin movie. So the next time they get in the
"phobic" situation, they go in the new direction.

	Just a little tingly feeling. Nothing like what I really have.
Richard	Did you see yourself in the image?
Lee	Yes, in a car, yeah. Looking out.
Richard	Looking out. Have you ever driven into the country?
Lee	Oh yeah.
Richard	Can you go back and remember it?
Lee	Yeah.
Richard	And when you remember can you see what you saw when it occurred?
Lee	You mean when I had a panic attack?
Richard	Yeah! You got it.
Lee	Okay. Well I thought you meant before.
Richard	No, I want to go for the full tilt here. See, I don't know. I have people come in and lie about having these problems.
Lee	No, I can remember the first one.
Richard	The very first one. Take you by surprise?
Lee	Yeah. I just turned snow white, my heart beating ninety miles an hour and just felt like I was going to die. I was going to pass out.

Richard   Is there any reason?

Lee   Not that I know of.

Richard   No deep psychological underpinnings to this?

Lee   No, not that I know of.

Richard   Just your brain went *arrgh* I've had enough. Scared the shit out of you?

Lee   Really.

Richard   Brains are like that. I have a theory about why. Did anybody ever tell you my theory?

Lee   No.

Richard   My theory is that the reason is, is because the world is tilted on its axis twenty degrees, so actually we each have someone else's brain and it's pissed.

Lee   (Laughter) Okay.

Richard   That's as much theory as I get into. It's the extent of my theoretical underpinnings. Okay. Would you go back and see what you saw and hear what you heard the very *first* time you had the panic attack?

Lee   I just came out of my uncle's house and got in my car. Started up the highway, the next thing I knew . . .

Richard   I want you to do it on the inside. I want you to
               actually see the same things you saw at that
               moment in time and hear the same sounds.

               (Pause)

Lee   Okay.

               (Pause)

Richard   Right up to the moment where you have it.

               (Pause)

Lee   Alright.

               (Pause)

Richard   Do you feel it when you do (lower tone) that?

Lee   Not like I did. But I feel something, yes.

Richard   Good. Is it intense?

Lee   Yeah.

Richard   Okay. I just wanted you to make sure you still
               had the problem. Sometimes people lose their
               problems. They're moving along in life and *boom*
               it's gone.

Lee   Well, it's not like it was. Not like it's actually
               being out there. It's a funny feeling. You can feel
               something that's telling you something there.

Richard   What do you think it's telling you?

Lee   Well, it's telling me what I went through and
                 what I'd go through again if I do it.

Richard   Maybe. Who knows? What do you think after
                 watching her?

Lee   Well, it's very interesting. Very, very interesting.
                 Kind of makes you believe . . . yeah.

Richard   Well, you see . . . the thing is, I have a really
                 good relationship with people's unconscious. I
                 don't seem to get along all that well with their
                 conscious minds most of the time. I know a lot
                 about how people learn. See, it's like if I reach
                 out to shake your hand, your hand knows how to
                 do that. After a while it kind of does it automati-
                 cally. And think of what a pain it would be if you
                 had to remember a handshake. Alright . . . life
                 hand up . . . if you had to relearn it so it just
                 quiiih . . . works automatically. So I like things to
                 be automatic. Somewhere along the line your
                 brain learned to panic outside the city limits. Now
                 if your brain can learn anything like that, I mean
                 maybe . . . it's trying to keep you here. It may
                 have a good reason. But by the same token, there
                 are other ways of doing that sort of thing. Seems
                 like that would be kind of inconvenient. Espe-
                 cially around here. Probably nice things outside
                 the city limits. What's out there?

Lee   Beautiful country for one thing. Jobs. When you
                 have to travel.

Richard   Jobs? Oh . . . well maybe there's part of you that
            would rather be poor and stuck in the city.

Lee   Maybe so . . .

Richard   Naw, I don't believe in that crap. Just can't buy
            into it. I know that we learn all kinds of things. It
            may have a function at one time, but after a while
            I don't think that those functions . . . imagine
            how many ridiculous things people learn that had
            a function at one time that don't any more. I
            always remember that there was a guy in one of
            my training seminars for nine months who was
            almost seven feet tall; he was a big man, but this
            training seminar took place in a room that only
            had three chairs and the rest were pillows and
            stuff. It was one of those places where they did
            encounter groups, and I rented the room from
            them. I had to sit in the chair. I don't like to sit
            on the floor. One day he walked up next to me
            and he looked at me and he went, "Boy," he said,
            "I always thought you were bigger than I was."
            Because on the inside he doesn't feel like he's
            seven feet tall. He feels much smaller than that.
            It's like he had forgotten. And people can forget
            stuff like that very easily. A lot of times people
            don't know that they've grown up. So on the
            inside they feel short, small, and all kinds of stuff.
            It's like, however you acquired it, it's really a
            fairly amazing thing that you can remember to
            panic. How many times have you gone outside
            the city limits and had this now? Do you remem-
            ber a number of times?

Lee	Probably like five to eight times.
Richard	How long ago did this happen?
Lee	The very first one was about two, two and a half years ago.
Richard	You've only tried eight times. How many ways are there out of the city?
Lee	Probably about six or eight.
Richard	See, I'm much more experimental than you. I would have tried all the different roads to see if you can escape. Because it might be your car.
Lee	I have the same car.
Richard	Did you take the same route all eight times?
Lee	No.
Richard	Good. Because there might be a sign out there that says, *"Don't Panic!"* Something nice like that. I had a friend who learned to have a marvelous thing because when he was young somebody in the medical profession told him he would have to learn to live with something that was wrong with him or jump off the Golden Gate Bridge. Lo and behold, about five years later they found a cure for it which hadn't existed until then. He found himself pacing up and down San Francisco near the Bridge, feeling suicidal for no reason. Now I'm sure the doctor had a good intention at that

time, but the person was just suggestible and it sort of stuck in there.

Lee   Just kept it in his mind.

Richard   It was a big thing to him. But anyway, tell you what I want you to do. Yours is a simple one. It's right up my alley. Nobody told you what my favorite thing was . . . my favorite thing is phobias because I don't have . . . I'm not endowed with a great memory. Sort of an airhead in many ways. I spend most of my life looking for where I just placed something. What I want you to do is . . . I want you to just simply go back and remember the time you left, was it your uncle's house?

Lee   Um huh.

Richard   Okay. Your uncle's house, and you know what you would see if you drove. How far is it?

Lee   Probably about seven miles.

Richard   Seven miles. That's okay. Then *wham* and, you know, at which point the panic hit. Because you can do it real fast in your head. See what you would see at the time you were there and all that stuff. Only this time what I want you to do is just to run through to make sure you have the memory. Only I want you to see yourself in the memory. In other words, watch as if you could fly next to the car, seeing the expression on your face. I want you to watch yourself through the experience. (long pause)

Lee	Alright.
Richard	Now when you see yourself, do you have any of those same kinds of feelings?
Lee	No, not really. I really don't. I see myself as a nervous wreck.
Richard	That's a bad word to use when you're talking about driving.
Lee	I know. I was. I was a nervous wreck.
Richard	You didn't wreck the car, did you?
Lee	No, I made it home.
Richard	But if you're not nervous you won't have to . . . in fact if you do get nervous I suggest you get calm. Have you ever thought about that?
Lee	I've tried to talk to myself. "Now just calm down here." But when you're in one of those, it's kind of hard to get out of it.
Richard	Yeah. It won't be. This time what I want you to do is . . . I want you to do it again. This time do it from the inside.
Lee	Just put myself right back where I was at?
Richard	Yeah, only this time you're going inside, and doing it from the inside. So you would begin to get those feelings that tell you that . . . (pause) You still feel them?

Lee   No, I really don't. I can think about it. I can pic-
             ture myself, how I got in the car and started out
             driving when it hit. But I *didn't* have that little
             tingling feeling I get when I think about it.

Richard   You didn't? Well . . .

             Just to be sure, I'll tell you what we're going to
             do. I want you to see it from the outside again,
             this time. I want you to run through it real fast
             and when you get to the end, the point just after
             you panic, the end of this particular memory, I
             want you to stop it as a slide. Then I want you to
             float as you would, see, from the outside of the
             car I want you to float to the inside so that you
             would see what you would see if you were there.
             And I want you to run the movie backwards until
             you're back at your uncle's house. You have to go
             all the way backwards. This is something that you
             really should do backwards.

             (Pause)

Lee   Alright.

Richard   Okay, now. Once again, I want you to run
             through it. See if you can find some of that panic
             in there. Wouldn't it be a bummer if it was this
             easy to change it? And you spent two years . . .

Lee   In counseling, yeah.

Richard   Well, you know what? That's what, nobody told
             you what to do. See, they go to school. They
             even do this thing sometimes in schools. They tell
             you that you have to spell. But they don't tell you

how. So a lot of people did it phonetically. Did you learn phonetics in school?

Lee   No.

Richard   Well you can't even spell "phonetics" phoneti-cally. Have you thought about that? Whoever made up the name for that system did not take themselves very seriously. When I went to school they taught me to spell phonically. Which meant that there are a lot of words that you can't spell phonetically. And the teachers can't spell well anyway. You go up and say, "How do you spell this word?" They always use the old cop-out, "Go look it up in the dictionary." If I knew how to spell it I could look it up in the dictionary in the first place. But most people stop and make a picture of the word. Then they copy it down. I didn't know people did that.

Lee   Me either.

Richard   That's what good spellers do. Now why don't they tell you that in school? And at school they didn't tell you that if you have a panic thing, stop, see yourself from the outside, run through the thing, make it into a slide and run it backwards. They don't tell you that. If somebody came along and did it . . . I was thinking of writing a survival handbook. Because I've decided that life causes death and that living creates great difficulties.

Lee   Yeah.

Richard	You wouldn't have problems if you weren't alive.
Lee	That's very true.
Richard	Suicidals have thought about that. They had a problem in that it wouldn't bother them if it wasn't . . . they wouldn't object to it if they hadn't been born in the first place. Go back and do it again. Let's see if we can get some panic out of you here.
	You're in big trouble, I'm getting warmed up.
Lee	No, I can think about it now and get that tingling feeling I usually get.
Richard	No tingling even? Oh, you can try harder than that. You can get to that tingling.
Lee	Well, I'll try.
	No, not really.
Richard	Oh come on. You want to be sure, don't you?
Lee	Yeah.
Richard	Okay. Then why don't we go for a ride out in the country?
Lee	I'm willing to try.
Richard	Stop and think about it. If you're willing to try.
	(Pause)
Lee	Yeah. What I said . . . I'm willing to try.

Richard   Well, that's different. We'll go for a ride here in a
             little while. I've got a couple other things I want
             to do, and then we'll go for a ride in the country.
             In fact, if it's only eight miles, maybe I can get
             somebody to take you out in the country and
             bring you back here. You can tell those folks out
             there in video land . . .

Lee   Just how it was for me. If when I really concen-
             trate hard about it I can get a sensation about it.
             But it's not like actually getting in a car and
             going.

Richard   Yeah, I know.

Lee   I can't bring myself to . . .

Richard   But you told me that when people asked you to
             go, you always said, "I can't."

Lee   Right.

Richard   You didn't say that because it's not true anymore.
             So we'll do that. Why don't we stop here and put
             it to the test?

             ————————————

Bill   It's been about one hour since Lee left the session
             with Dr. Bandler to go out and to see what would
             happen now with his phobic response of driving
             outside the city limits. He's arriving back in the
             studio to share what that experience was for him.

Richard	Okay. Lee has just come back here, and I thought I'd have you report what happened.
Lee	I went out of the city limits and I went out of the state.
Richard	You went out of the state!
Lee	Just across the bridge, yeah. It's about two miles from here, three miles.
Richard	What bridge?
Lee	Sixth Street Bridge in Huntington, Chesapeake, Ohio.
Richard	Got out in the country, then?
Lee	Well, it's out of the city limits, I'll guarantee you that. It's a small town over there. I even thought about it crossing the bridge and everything.
Richard	How long has it been since you've been across that bridge?
Lee	Four and a half years.
Richard	Four and a half years. Well, what do you think about that?
Lee	I just can't believe it happened to me. It's like getting out of prison. Is this really happening? That's about what it amounts to. Always before when I've tried to go outside the city limits, I kept waiting for this panic attack. Some of the time it

happened, most of the time it didn't. This time I didn't even . . . I wasn't even waiting for it to happen. I just went over and came back.

Richard   How long has it been since you've been on a vacation?

Lee   Oh gee, at least six, seven years. I really want to take one, but I can't. I wanted to go to the World's Fair with my family . . .

Richard   You can go now.

Lee   Yeah.

Richard   Is that where you're going to go, the World's Fair?

Lee   If they don't close up by the time I get down there.

Richard   How long is it going to run?

Lee   I think it runs through . . .

Richard   They run it for a whole year, don't they?

Lee   No, I think it's only October, I believe.

Richard   Better get in the car and get going.

Lee   Really.

Richard   Where else? How do you think . . . what do you think's going to happen when you go home?

Lee	They're not going to believe me. So I'll take them somewhere. My family.
Richard	You're going to take them somewhere this evening?
Lee	I believe I will.
Richard	Take them for a drive. You'll probably have to do that to convince them.
Lee	Oh yeah, I will.
Richard	Then you'll probably have to tell them that you've been tied to posts and had nails driven into your head. People don't think change should be very easy.
Lee	Yeah, I didn't think it would be that easy.
Richard	What was it like for you to have it be that simple?
Lee	You just don't believe it. You just can't comprehend that you actually can do it.
Richard	Thank you.
Lee	Thank you.
Richard	You're welcome. Have a good time. It's a big world out there.
Lee	Yeah, I guess it is. I'm going to find out about it, too.

Richard	Maybe some time you'll even make it out to the west. But don't drive to where I live.
Lee	Be kind of hard, wouldn't it?
Richard	That's right. It's a long drive through the ocean.

Conclusion

In Lee's case it didn't take a six-month follow-up to know the effect of the session. All it took was the trip out of town to convince Lee that he was capable of doing something he never thought he would do.

His willingness to get into the car and drive is actually more important than the fact that he did it. Lee couldn't even think about it before; his mind wouldn't let him consider it, but now he was excited to go. That's the change. He didn't say, "Oh, that's hard." There was no hesitation. It's the lack of effort that is crucial. He didn't turn around and "face" his problem; he just drove out of the state and had a Coke.

With this in mind, I knew Lee's phobic response wouldn't come back. What he needed now was a way to deal with the problems that would arise from this new situation. He needed a way to enable his family and friends to account for the quick change and take advantage of the opportunity to open up new possibilities, rather than analyze his old difficulties.

In NLP we describe this as "ecology." It's just common sense that when people suddenly make dramatic changes they have been trying to make for years, they are going to hear a lot of "I told you so." This is another reason it's important to orient people in the future; otherwise they go back and have regrets about all the years they've wasted.

Sometimes I tell clients just to say that the Lord healed them and leave it at that. Most people won't argue with the Lord's ability to create fast and pervasive change.

Chapter 3

Fear of Authority Figures

This case puts the client, Michael, in a paradoxical situation right from the start. He wants to overcome his difficulty with authority figures, but he has to deal with me; quite frankly, I'm capable of acting like an authority figure like no one you've ever seen.

Michael, like Susan, has the ability to create fear before an event occurs and to maintain an association based on past experiences—to have what he refers to as a "yuck feeling" in these contexts. In working with Michael I directly use his ability to create these responses.

Another crucial element in this case, as in any of my client sessions, is humor. Although the transcripts do not reflect the humorous tonality I use with clients, it has always been my best tool for getting people to laugh in the face of their fears. When human beings learn to laugh at their problems, they can do something about them!

I'll do anything—from telling clients jokes to making faces at them—that reduces the intensity of the overwhelming feelings they experience.

In Michael's case I use humor to reduce the impact of the pictures that produce his "yuck feeling" and thus enable him to master these feelings and start doing things in more useful ways.

I've often been told that my language is foul and my techniques are crass, but I've found that with human beings, blunt works best. I would not be able to criticize clients if I wasn't convinced that their lives could be so much better, easier and more richly lived.

Clients aren't broken, and there is no need to treat them as if they were. They work fine, but the question is, are they *happy* with how they work? If they can learn to have difficulty, then they can learn to respond differently.

In the following transcript Michael demonstrates that not only is there nothing wrong with him but that he is extremely educatable, if you can show him a way to take control of his internal states.

Bill   This is one of a series of video tapes featuring Richard Bandler who is the co-originator and developer of Neuro-Linguistic Programming. With me is Michael Saggese serving as narrator, and Michael we've certainly been extremely fortunate to have Dr. Bandler in this series.

Michael   Bill, I think it's a real unique opportunity to be able to have Dr. Bandler in a studio situation where we can do high quality tapes as well as be able to provide follow up of those tapes eight months down the road. I'm real excited about this project.

Bill   I think that is a unique feature. We've both had a lot of experience doing clinical work in which you work with someone in an audience or you work with someone in your office and you really never know whether what you did was effective. This is often true of professionals. We're going to have the uniqueness here that eight months later we're going to interview the people that Dr. Bandler worked with.

Michael   Not only that Bill, it's been my experience and I think yours too that many of the training tapes I saw as a student, as a graduate trainee, you saw someone work with a subject and then the tape ended but you never knew what happened to them. And I think the fact that we have decided to make this project to go back and look eight months later at the follow up lends something to this tape that's kind of unique.

Bill   Yes. We have a manual that goes with the video tape and we're going to be explaining to people more in depth about Neuro-Linguistic Programming. But would you take just a minute to tell people watching the tapes what Neuro-Linguistic Programming is. Could you just speak to that a moment, maybe how is it different from other approaches that are often used in therapy.

Michael   I think there's a lot of answers to that question
               Bill. For me the most distinguishing thing that I
               find exciting is the fact that NLP, although it is a
               model, and a modeling process, offers us an
               opportunity to begin to understand the internal
               structure of someone's experience. And as you
               will notice on the various tapes, you'll see Dr.
               Bandler beginning to work with someone's inter-
               nal experience.

Bill   Rather than looking simply at externally what
               their behavior is.

Michael   Precisely. For instance, he may begin to, in one
               situation, examine someone's internal images, or
               someone's internal auditor . . . how they talk to
               themselves. And as we will see and hear on these
               tapes those internal experiences, the structure of
               those experiences has a tremendous impact and
               influence on their feelings as well as their external
               behavior.

Bill   One of the amazing things for me that I enjoy
               time after time watching is that as you watch
               Mike in this tape working with Dr. Bandler, that
               the body itself tells you what's happening
               internally. Particularly one of the things that Dr.
               Bandler has helped discover in terms of eye
               movements. As people began to internally make
               pictures their eyes move upward. You can watch
               Mike in this tape as he visualizes things, you can
               watch his eyes move up to make those pictures.
               Dr. Bandler comments about that several times.

Michael   I think one of the uniquenesses of NLP is that
             since it's based on sensory information, how peo-
             ple process information, there are cues that you
             can use. Like eye movements. We call them eye
             accessing movements. Most people access visual
             images by looking up. Most people access
             auditory information by looking somewhere else.

Bill   In other words, when they're talking to
             themselves?

Michael   When they're talking to themselves or talking
             externally very often. As well as people will move
             their eyes in a different direction when they're
             feeling something. The fact that you as an
             observer, can begin to notice this gives you an
             indication of how the individual you're working
             with is processing information.

Bill   So as we're watching this tape one of the things
             that the person learning about NLP should look
             for . . . one of the times here he finds out that
             Mike is doing something very unique that's creat-
             ing a problem for him. That is while he's dealing
             with people externally, he's talking to himself
             internally. He really discovers that by watching his
             eye movements.

Michael   What's fascinating about it, if you watch the tape
             closely, is Dr. Bandler discovers that before Mike
             discovers it.

Bill   Yes. Anything else the people should look for in
             this tape?

Michael   The thing I would ask them to use their senses
                 enough to listen for and to look for, are also Dr.
                 Bandler's unique interaction with this individual
                 as well as notice the changes that Mike begins to
                 experience. You may notice facial gestures, eye
                 movements or his level of comfortableness or
                 tenseness in his body as he begins to continually
                 interact with Dr. Bandler.

Bill   Dr. Bandler really seems to be having a good time
                 and at times almost playing games with this partic-
                 ular client. How would you explain that?

Michael   One of the things that I've learned, and I think
                 you've learned too from our personal experience
                 with Dr. Bandler is that he always knows what
                 he's doing. And one of the things we would cau-
                 tion though it looks very simple as Dr. Bandler
                 does this. He's using some very sophisticated NLP
                 techniques as he interacts with Michael. I believe
                 he's using humor as a way of helping Michael
                 relax and developing rapport with him and giving
                 him also more and more information about
                 Michael as he interacts with him.

Bill   Yes. So we're very very happy to introduce to
                 you Dr. Bandler as he works with Michael.

                 ───────────

Richard   Okay now. What's your name? Your name is
                 Michael, right?

Mike   Mike, right.

Richard	I can remember that because I thought you were somebody else earlier.
Mike	Right. There are enough Michaels.
Richard	I figure if you use Michael, Richard, Bob, Gary and a few names like that you've got a one in ten chance of saying the right name anyway, especially with Catholics. You can't miss with Catholics.
Mike	Pat, Mike.
Richard	Yes. Pat, Mike, sort of narrows it down. Okay, so what brings you here? You just weren't walking down the hall; you obviously want something.
Mike	Right. Some behaviors that I run on myself.
Richard	Run on yourself? Now that's a new one. I haven't had anybody who runs on themselves. Come on, give me a hint. I'm not a good guesser. I don't know. They don't tell me anything ahead of time.
Mike	I run feelings that are unpleasant. And I want to get away from them.
Richard	Which ones? Any particular ones or are we just going to . . .
Mike	Anxiety, fear, a yuck feeling in my stomach.
Richard	Are these different feelings, or do you run them all together?
Mike	Run them together.

Richard	You run them together. How do you know when to do it?
Mike	When I'm in the right situation. The situation says it's time to do it, or I say to myself it's time to do it.
Richard	If I had to do it, let's say that I had to do this, how would I know which situations I was going to do it in as opposed to which ones I wouldn't? You have to know when to have your problem. It's like disappointment, it requires adequate planning.
Mike	Yes. So how would you know when to do it? Ok. Specifically you get the feeling first, you get . . .
Richard	No . . . you have to know when to have the feeling. You're not just walking down the street and get struck down with the yuck feeling.
Mike	In talking with, communicating with authority figures.
Richard	Oh, with authority figures. Hey, we can test this one, can't we? How come you want to change this? What's so bad about feeling bad? How would your life be different if you didn't have the yuck feeling?
Mike	Because I could communicate more effectively with those who I want to communicate with.
Richard	Maybe. At least you'd be more comfortable when you did.

Mike   Oh I'd be more comfortable.

Richard   So when you communicate with authority
              figures, how do you know which people are
              authority figures?

              First you have to make a complicated decision: is
              this an authority figure? And then you can know
              to feel the yuck or not.

Mike   Those people who are in a position of some
              power with respect to my situation, like a sales
              manager at the office.

Richard   People who sign checks?

Mike   Yes. The boss.

Richard   I'll tell you a funny story. I recently broke my arm
              and I have a stick shift in the car and I couldn't
              drive to a meeting of entrepreneurs for a business
              thing. So I hired a limousine to have the driver
              drive me down and went to my meetings then
              drove back where I had to go. The driver was a
              black guy and he had on his little suit and stuff.
              We were talking and he took his hat off, threw it
              down and he came in and helped me clean up my
              office a little bit because I had been gone. We
              were kind of talking and we had a cocktail and
              then the two guys showed up. One guy was presi-
              dent of a very, very large corporation who has
              recently left that position and wants to be
              involved in a smaller business because he's 60
              some odd years old now. Another guy that's a
              millionaire and there was supposed to be another

person coming. They assumed that the black chauffeur was the big bucks millionaire from Texas. They kept talking to him and stuff, and he said, "I know you guys have to talk and stuff, so I'm going to go down to the cafe and I'll sit and have coffee until you guys are done," and left. This guy who was president of the company turned around and he said, "God I blew it. What did I do?" And I said, "Blew what?" And he said, "I just blew the whole deal." I said, "What are you talking about?" He says, "That was the guy from Texas." I said, "No it wasn't." And you see, he had had all these bad feelings and it had been a mistake. So when you have your yuck feeling you have to be a little bit more careful. How do you make the yuck feeling? You can't just . . . poof . . . have the feeling. You have to do something. You have to make a few pictures first, or something, don't you?

Mike   I talk to myself.

Richard   What kinds of things do you say?

Mike   Oh my God. I'm starting to feel this way.

Richard   Don't you make pictures . . . something terrible happening? Do you see yourself with this person internally or what? You have to do something.

Mike   I'm not sure what I do.

Richard   That's why I'm here. I have to get you to stop and figure out how to do it.

Mike	OK, I'll figure it out.
Richard	Or you don't get your check.
Mike	It seems to me like I talk to myself first.
Richard	What kind of things do you say?
Mike	Oh my God. I want out of this situation.
Richard	But how do you know you want out of it?
Mike	I want to get away from the feeling.
Richard	Before you have the feeling, so you have to back up. You have to have something to make the yuck out of. Do you see yourself being small? Do you have the yuck going into the situation?
Mike	Yes.
Richard	See, we're backing up here.
Mike	Okay.
Richard	How do you know when to start yucking? When's the last time you did this?
Mike	This morning.
Richard	When did you start feeling yuck this morning?
Mike	After the phone rang, and I was into a conversation.

Richard   When it rang there was somebody on the other
             end?

Mike   Yes.

Richard   You didn't want to be talking to that person?

Mike   Oh I did, and I didn't.

Richard   You did, and you didn't?

Mike   Right.

Richard   How do you know you didn't? Did you begin to
             see that something was . . .

Mike   I wanted to communicate a situation to him
             which was unpleasant for me and I was not really
             wanting to do for fear of his response.

Richard   Did you see him responding badly?

Mike   No.

Richard   Is it tone?

Mike   No. It seems to me like it's a fear.

Richard   When you have a fear how do you know which
             fear of . . . this morning you were afraid of what
             happening?

Mike   Okay, I was afraid of what.

Richard   You don't go around being afraid of chairs, pieces
             of tile.

Mike	Fear of losing a friend.
Richard	Did you see him actually . . . I mean, how did you know you were going to lose him? Did you tell yourself?
Mike	I was telling myself.
Richard	You're making pictures now. I can see you making pictures. As many pictures as you've been making here, I just know that you had to be making some. So what were you making pictures of when you were talking to him?
Mike	Pictures of myself?
Richard	You saw yourself talking to him? That's probably why you dressed so neatly. You can see yourself. The gentleman who was up here before couldn't see himself in the car that much . . . see himself being afraid. When he saw himself it's different. It's real different to see yourself in a situation. Try this. Can you see yourself riding in the front seat of a roller coaster?
Mike	Yes.
Richard	See what you would see if you were actually there.
Mike	Yes.
Richard	Are they different?
Mike	Yes.

Richard   How are they different?

Mike   When I'm seeing what I'm seeing when I'm there
            I am in the . . . I am looking from (with a shaky
            voice).

Richard   You have the feelings of being on a roller coaster?

            (Mimicking Mike's voice) Somewhat.

            Okay. Whereas if you see yourself there it's like
            watching someone else be on a roller coaster?

Mike   Yes.

Richard   If you go back and remember and see and hear
            the same thing that you saw an heard at the
            time . . . that's alright, don't worry about it . . .
            see and hear the same thing that occurred the last
            time you had this. Then do you get back the same
            kind of yuck feeling?

Mike   No. Or vaguely. Not to the extent that I can
            remember it.

Richard   But if you go back to the conversation, or pick
            just the worst example of feeling yuck you can
            think of. Just the most really intense example you
            can find and see and hear the same thing you saw
            and heard at the time it was occurring. You can
            close your eyes if you want to really get into it.

            Can you get back the feelings too when you do
            that? Do you hear the same things you heard then?

Mike   Part of it.

Richard   Well you can't leave out part.

Mike   I was talking but I don't remember what I was saying. If I were hearing what I was hearing I would hear myself talking and hear words. I can get back the tone of my voice more than actually what was . . .

Richard   Do you know what you were seeing at the time?

Mike   Perhaps myself.

Richard   Perhaps!

Mike   Alright. Myself.

Richard   If you see yourself and you're watching yourself while you're talking out loud, do you talk internally at the same time?

Mike   Um huh.

Richard   You've got two fucking conversations going on. No wonder you don't remember what you said. Have you ever said the wrong thing?

Mike   Yes.

Richard   It's probably because you weren't listening on the outside. You were listening on the inside. You can get in a lot of trouble with women doing that. Because they hear every word. Has it ever occurred to you to stop talking on the inside and listen to yourself on the outside?

Mike   Yes.

Richard   It's not easy, is it?

Mike   No.

Richard   How would you like to feel instead of yuck?

Mike   Confident. In control.

Richard   Of what?

Mike   Myself. My voice.

Richard   You don't have to have control to do that, you just have to listen.

Mike   Okay.

Richard   Is it that you want to be confident? Confidence is a boring feeling as far as I'm concerned. How would you like to feel when you're in a situation?

Mike   How would I like to feel?

Richard   Let's say I had a bag of feelings and I could make it, for example, that when you're in that situation, you'd have any feeling you wanted. You came in here and asked to not have certain feelings. I do that with a knife. I can make it so you'll never have any of those feelings again. We go out behind the building, I take the knife, I slit your throat and you'll never feel it again. It's very permanent and it works too.

Mike   We won't do that.

Richard   Okay, we'll skip over that one then. When people
             say they want to not have a certain feeling, of
             course they don't have any of the rest of them.

Mike   I don't want those feelings in certain situations.

Richard   Good. You might like to keep them around for
             other situations. We have to put something in its
             place. If I'm going to be the one that chooses, I'll
             pick terror, unadulterated, trembling terror. And
             I'll come out with another good tape. But what
             would you like? Confidence is kind of ehhh.

Mike   I don't like that.

Richard   How would you like to feel? What would be the
             most useful feeling that you know of?

Mike   Exhilarated, excited.

Richard   You want it to be fun you mean?

Mike   Yes.

Richard   I find I like the more juicy ones. Exhilarated
             sounds so intellectual.

Mike   How would you like for it to sound?

Richard   What kind of feelings do you have when you're
             thrilled and exhilarated? Kind of get down greasy
             at the same time.

             Yeah, that one there. I like that one. That's a
             good one, we're going to hold on to that. You go
             back and pick the worst example one again. You

must have seen something at the time it was
occurring.

Mike   Um huh.

Richard   Alright. See what you saw and go back and listen.
              Just take this with you. (R. anchors by pressing
              Mike's foot with his hand.) That's right. Close
              your eyes. Begin to run through different times
              and places and memories. Between each one go
              back to the one that gave you this feeling.
              Exhilarated plus.

              That's right. Keep this with you. Should take that
              everywhere you go. Makes your skin glow pretty.
              You've got some playful parts in there. I can see.
              They sneak out when you drink don't they?

Mike   Yes.

Richard   They do. I thought they did. Somebody once told
              me life was too serious and I told them, I said, in
              the game of life there are no conscientious objec-
              tors. When they deal a hand they may not do it
              twice but it doesn't mean you can't deal from the
              bottom of the deck. Some cards up the sleeve and
              you can take the worst of situations and make
              them into something fun.

              Did you go back to that feeling between each of
              the memories? Go back to the memory that . . .
              Can you think of a time when you were in . . .
              when I asked about something that's exhilarating
              and a little get down greasy. That one there. Do
              you know what memory that is? Don't tell us out
              loud, this is not an R-rated film.

Michael   Yes.

Richard   Okay then what I want you to do is take that (R.
             activates anchor). If you were that person, can
             you see yourself being that way in these situa-
             tions? Take the way you act in that and see your-
             self being that way in these kinds of situations. If
             you have this feeling, the feeling of . . . let's give
             it a name . . . exhilaration plus. Sounds like a new
             vitamin.

Mike   Right.

Richard   I took exhilaration plus every day. Take that one,
             exhilaration plus, and see yourself being that kind
             of person in a couple of the past experiences you
             had. In other words, go back. We call this change
             history. If you don't like your past make up a new
             one. All criminals know about that.

Mike   Right.

Richard   Go back and change a couple of them. Watch
             yourself go through those. See if you like the way
             you would act. It's alright to amuse yourself too in
             these constructions. Just close your eyes. Let your
             imagination run away with you. That's when life
             is it's best anyway.

             You like the way that looks? Smirking is allowed.

Mike   Yes.

Richard   You do? How would you like to have that? I'm
             having a sale here today.

Mike	(With a flat voice) I'd like it.
Richard	You sound so enthusiastic about it. Is that what you'd like? You have to be careful because I give people these things.
Mike	Umm, okay. Well I'm not sure. Maybe not. I want something different.
Richard	Okay. Well why don't you go in there and change it till you get it the way you like it?
Mike	Okay.
Richard	Don't be too reserved.
Mike	Alright. (Pause)
Richard	The guy before you is now on vacation somewhere. (Pause)
Mike	I'm not sure what I want.
Richard	You had two seconds to decide. You don't know what you want?
Mike	Right.
Richard	That's okay. It's kind of like an adventure then, isn't it? You would like to be different in a whole bunch of them. In other words, make an image of yourself the way you are now in one of those sit-uations. Nice big bright picture in your head.

Complete with sound and motion. I put music
with some of mine.

Mike   Circus music.

Richard   Circus music! It's exactly what I do most of the
            time. Keeps my sense of humor up. You keep
            looking at that image and then step inside the
            image and see if you can recapture the feeling. In
            other words can you still feel yuck?

Mike   A little.

Richard   A little? Oh come on, go back and try and get it.
            Do you feel any of exhilaration? Plus?

Mike   No.

Richard   Oops. I'm being attacked in here. By the
            microbes . . . beep beep. No what?

Mike   No I don't feel exhilaration plus.

Richard   You don't huh. Okay. Do you feel . . . can you
            go back and get a hold of yuck? Could you still
            feel yuck?

Mike   I don't feel it now.

Richard   Well could you?

Mike   Could I in the future feel it?

Richard   Maybe some time and some place. I'm not a ther-
            apist by the way. Therapists have intuitions. I just
            lie. I go, I have an intuition. You're wearing a

brown jacket. I have an intuition that you're going to have some difficulty feeling it.

Mike   Good.

Richard   Why don't you, right now, stop a second and see if you can go inside and create a situation in which you would know that, if you even thought about it, you'd know that you were going to feel?

Mike   Okay.

Richard   See if you can go in and make some yuck.

Mike   (Replies immediately) No.

Richard   You didn't try very hard, come on. What was that, a two second try? I'm going to test my work here you know. You've got to get in there and fight to have those bad feelings.

Mike   Alright.

Richard   After all, you were the master of it. Weren't you?

Mike   Yes. (tries again)
            Nope.

Richard   Can't do it?

Mike   Right.

Richard   Okay. Let's stop here. It was a pleasure. Thank you.

———————

Bill   It's been approximately eight months since Dr.
                Bandler worked with Mike and dealing with
                authority figures and perhaps some other interest-
                ing sidelines to that. This is a follow up of that
                particular session. We have Mike with us today.
                Glad to welcome you here. We wanted to have a
                chance after this period of time to find out what
                Dr. Bandler had done from your perspective and
                what kind of things had been effective for you.
                And maybe Mike (Saggese, the editor) would like
                to kind of set the stage for that and ask the first
                question.

Michael   Mike, as you look back on the work that you did
                with Dr. Bandler, for you what was the most
                important thing that you learned that happened
                during that session?

Mike   That what was causing the problem I wanted to
                change was an internal conversation at the time
                that I was trying to do something else.

Michael   As a result of having that internal conversation
                with yourself, what happened?

Mike   I didn't deal as I wanted to deal with what I was
                doing externally, like talking with other people.
                And I also would end up having some very nega-
                tive feelings about the situation.

Bill   So let me see if I understand that. It was really a
                unique discovery for you to find out that when
                you're dealing with people out here, inside you

were talking to yourself. Is that a unique discovery for you?

Mike   Yes.

Bill   Because I noticed as we watched the tape there are a number of times you're, he's asking you what it is you do and you say I don't know what I do. And then when he said are you talking to yourself, that's when you became aware of it?

Mike   Right.

Michael   As a result of making this discovery, how has it affected your interaction with other people at this point in time?

Mike   It's improved it. It's made it a more comfortable situation to get in the situations that I want to get into without all the negative feelings.

Michael   Now we're eight months down the road. Are you finding that the discovery you made, that it's still helpful to you?

Mike   Definitely.

Michael   By discovering the fact that you're trying to carry on two conversations simultaneously and interrupting actually with one conversation, the externally one, that discovery has helped you to interact more effectively with other people?

Mike   Yes.

Bill	Have there been any things that you didn't expect? You knew what you found that day, but helping you deal with authority figures is one area. Have you found it helped you with other people?
Mike	Yes.
Bill	Any particular ones?
Mike	Groups of people. Speaking in front of groups.
Bill	Oh, okay. Public speaking made a difference too. You mean before you tried to speak before an audience that you often had an internal conversation going about how you were doing or what you might be doing?
Mike	Or I shouldn't get upset now because I was going to speak in front of a group.
Bill	I've had an occasion a time or two to watch you speak before an audience and that didn't seem to be happening. You seem to be handling yourself well. So you've been using that?
Mike	Yes.
Michael	I'd like to mention the fact that there will be a manual coming out in relation to the tape. I'd also like to mention that Bill and I will be available to do training and other people as well as Richard. Is there anything you'd like to add?

Bill   Well, I think one of the things as people watch
                the tape it seems so simple to watch what Dr.
                Bandler was doing that one might be tempted to
                say, well I can do that. We really would like to
                give a word of caution. Do not attempt to do
                NLP until you've had some training and some
                knowledge in that area. People would find it
                exciting to learn that, but they would find it not
                quite as easy as Dr. Bandler sometimes makes it
                appear.

Michael   Yes, it is. And that addresses about where they can
                get in touch with us or Dr. Bandler will be avail-
                able at the end of the tape.

Bill   Yes. Mike, thank you for being with us today.
                We enjoyed having you come back after this long
                period of time. Very happy to find out that your
                session with Dr. Bandler was worth the time. It
                was a successful adventure for you.

Conclusion

All three clients discussed so far were considered therapeutic
impossibilities and had been in treatment for up to eight years.
All three were treated in less than 30 minutes.

The important thing is not whether they are treated in 30 minutes or 30 sessions; the important thing is that, rather than just
overcoming a problem, they are able to take a new direction in
life, to change their focus from what is impossible to what is
possible. Turning around a difficulty quickly and easily becomes

a reference point that can improve every aspect of their lives to which they are willing to generalize it.

I want NLP practitioners to understand that NLP is not so much a remedial as a generative model. The goal for an NLP practitioner should not be to overcome a phobia but to reorient clients, so that instead of living with fear they move through life with hope and a sense of adventure. When they return for follow-up sessions, their question should be, "What is possible for me and how can I go for it with enjoyment and quickly?" rather than, "What do I need to get over next?"

Chapter 4

Chocolate and Worms

The following chapters are transcripts of seminar demonstrations. The participants had come to learn NLP as well as to overcome some personal difficulties.

"Chocolate and Worms" offers good examples of submodality manipulation in controlling internal states. It shows how a craving for chocolate or a fear of worms, which had been pervasive phenomena in Eileen's and Anita's lives respectively, very quickly cease to be problems once they learn how to use their minds and realize the meaning of the statement, "It's all in your head."

Again, I'd like to emphasize that I'm not just interested in helping someone overcome a particular problem. I would consider treating a craving for chocolate or a fear of worms a waste of time if I didn't use it as an opportunity to demonstrate how limitations can be abolished with laughter and to direct the person to something in life that is more rewarding. With all the possibilities human beings have to get creatively and passionately involved in life, people shouldn't have to spend their time avoiding worms or fighting a desire for chocolate.

One reason therapists often have trouble getting simple results is that they're obsessed with them. If they could cure somebody of a phobia, then they could go on to look for the next problem. I don't think phobias are a problem to begin with; if I can use phobias as examples of how people can take control of their brains, they'll solve their other difficulties and start focusing on much more interesting things.

My goal is not for clients never to have their problems again. I want them to have the attitude that "I can when I want to— I know how to turn it off and how to turn it on." This gives them a much greater goal: to be able to run their own brains and their own lives.

Love of Chocolate

Richard   The first question is, what's your name?

Eileen   Eileen.

Richard   Now Eileen, you said prior to starting you crave chocolate against your will, how do you know when to have a craving for chocolate?

Eileen   I don't know when to have a craving for chocolate. It just happens.

Richard   Oh. This is separate from the rest of life. You see, if I had told you that I had to have cravings for chocolate, what would make me crave chocolate?

Eileen	I don't know what makes me crave chocolate. It just appears. It just happens.
Eileen	I see it, I taste it, I smell it, I see myself enjoying it. Ahhhhhh.
Richard	It sure does, look at the glow on her face. Whew!
Group	(Laughter) . . . Ahhhhhh . . . Get down! . . . Godiva chocolate?
Richard	Let's attach that to her husband. (Laughter)
Eileen	I can do that too.
Richard	So immediately, that'd be nice. A glow like that, she'd have a marriage that would last forever.
Eileen	Sixteen years. (Laughter)
Richard	You look at that image. You did the exercise where you turned things up and down. Right? If you turned up the brightness of the image, did it intensify your feelings? You look like one of those. Some people turn up the brightness and it diminishes their feelings. Some people it doesn't have any effect at all. Did you have a big bright picture of chocolate? Okay. What happens if you turn the brightness down?
Eileen	Looks like a big chocolate advertisement. Like old chocolate.
Richard	Turn it down even further.

Eileen   Something like a picture in a black and white
            newspaper advertisement of chocolate.

Richard   Okay. Let's go to the other thing. Again this is the
            same as cigarettes. It's no different. Chocolate and
            cigarettes are two of the major habits in this world
            as far as I can tell. What happens if you're in a
            room where people are eating chocolate? You
            have to remember there's both the inside and the
            outside. Do you crave . . .

Eileen   I don't crave it if other people are eating it. I
            enjoy watching them eat it. But I may not have
            the craving at the same time.

Richard   Okay. For a lot of people it doesn't work that
            way. These are things we need to know.
            Especially with smokers. Light up a cigarette. I
            like to, when discussing smoking, smoke. And
            whenever I work with somebody about smoking I
            always smoke. In fact that's how I started
            smoking. (Laughter) It's called stealing behavior.
            A lot of people, when you light up a cigarette . . .
            boom . . . they reach for the package. But it
            doesn't seem to work that way for you. Now how
            do we take all these pieces about what we know
            and get it so now we know that whatever it is that
            triggers it, there's a point in time where you get
            this big bright image? If you had a conscious mind
            which was somewhat diligent when it saw that
            image, it would just turn it down. This requires
            cooperation of your conscious mind, which is not
            always that cooperative as far as I can tell about
            conscious minds. But if you do it right now and

turned it down again the same thing happens. If you pulled the pleasure out, what would be a way of . . . if we think about it, of getting it to do that by itself? If she thinks of chocolate in the brightness of the image, then automatically so that the intensity . . .

Group   How about anchoring?

Richard   That is anchoring. Anchoring, as far as I'm concerned, is old. Old stuff. What we're doing here is a form of anchoring which is much more methodical. The old anchoring is very useful for some things. But this is like the high-powered stuff. That image that she has is an anchor. But it's not only an anchor, it's one you can turn up and down. What we want to do is to get it, when it is there, to turn down by itself. The best way to do that is to get something else turning up. So what we do is ask questions: why not just eat chocolate all the time?

Eileen   It would make me sick.

Richard   That's true, it would make you sick. Is there any other reason? Why would you want to diminish your enjoyment of, or your pleasure and attraction to chocolate? We'll wait here for a few minutes . . . for you to figure out a good reason. (Laughter)

Eileen   I don't like the taste of chocolate that much, but I want to eat that much of it or for that long. It would make me sick.

Other	If you make it too regular of a thing, it would lose its desirability?
Richard	You're the one that brought it up here. Are you content with your chocolate consumption? It's not something you want to change in your life? I don't want to wreck something pleasant here.
Eileen	What I'm not content with is the craving that comes. I don't want the craving. I can choose or not choose when to eat chocolate. But I don't like that craving. I get the feeling that I no longer can choose . . . it sort of like overwhelms me and takes over and *I HAVE GOT TO HAVE CHOCOLATE!!*
Richard	Do you actually go get some?
Eileen	Yes.
Richard	Oh, then you don't have the choice at that point?
Eileen	That's what I mean.
Richard	Then what is it that you don't like about that? When you get into those things where you have to have it and you eat it.
Eileen	It's a feeling of being out of control. Not having an active part in what I do or don't do.
Richard	Are there any negative side effects?
Eileen	I feel very out of control.

Richard   Now we're talking.

Eileen   My stomach gets upset. I eat too much.

Richard   Okay. Moving right along here. When you're in control, the side effects are that your skin looks better, you . . .

Eileen   I don't feel sick to my stomach.

Richard   You feel and you look better. If you have an image of, for example, when you in your mind get into a state where you're "AHHHHHHH I'VE GOT TO HAVE CHOCOLATE," that kind of state, do you have, at that point in time, an image of what you're like when you're in control? In other words, you want to have control in this. If you really had control over this, how do you think you would look and feel? Obviously something attracts you to bring this up in the first place.

Eileen   Well, I just don't like being out of control over chocolate.

Richard   Do you think you would look and sound and feel better?

Eileen   Oh sure.

Richard   Do you have an image of that? Do you have a picture of that? Now, turn that one up. Make it *brighter*. Make it even *brighter*. Make it a little bit *brighter* still. Does that increase the pleasant feeling that goes with that?

Eileen   (Ecstatically) It really does.

Richard   We're going to try a little game here. This is sci-
             ence, mind you. What I want you to do is follow
             me. I want you to take the chocolate, the bright
             chocolate image. The really bright chocolate
             image . . . not yet, I'll tell you when . . . jumped
             on your chocolate image and ate it up! . . . I want
             you to do something like this, just as an experi-
             ment. I want you to take that image . . . I don't
             know what your images are. Some people's
             images are square, some people's are hexagrams,
             but whatever it is I want you to put down, in the
             corner of it, this small image. Sort of a dark, small
             image of the second one, where you look and feel
             better and are more in control. But make this one
             bright. What I want you to do is to make this
             image get darker and smaller, and this image here
             get brighter and bigger. I want you to just go
             inside and do that mechanically five times and
             then shut it off. Don't go back the other way. Do
             you understand? In other words, don't reverse
             them. Stop, open your eyes, and come out and
             come back in. Make the image again and make it
             go that way.

Eileen   Going from small, dark . . .

Richard   Having the choice and everything. With a great
             big "desire for chocolate" image. Then this one
             gets darker and smaller and this one gets lighter
             and bigger. Then you end there and come out. I
             want you to do that five times in a row . . .
             That's one . . . That's right. Okay, now, by the

way, those of you back there with note pads . . . for those of you who are learning to see skin color changes, that's really where it's going on. I've learned that if I pick people in the back corner, other people watch with their hips turned. Now, what I want you to do is . . . this time I want you to just go in and make a chocolate image and find out what happens on its own.

Eileen   I can't do that.

Richard   *Sure you can.* Nice big bright chocolate image. Oh, try once more just for me. You can try it a little harder just one more time.

Eileen   I can't. Mud, just muddy.

Richard   Oh, you can try it a little harder. One more time, try.

Eileen   I can't. Mud, all mud.

Richard   And how do you feel about losing your compulsion? (sarcastic) That's called grief repair. (Laughter from group)

Eileen   How do you do that with cigarettes?

Richard   Oh that doesn't work with cigarettes. You see, Eileen you're going to win your bet, aren't you? Do you know that now? Remember you asked me yesterday at lunch?

Eileen   (Giggling) Oh that . . . I had a bet . . .

Richard   That's why I told you it wouldn't work. Still I
             want to bet some money on it, DON'T BE
             FOOLISH.

Eileen   I don't smoke so I don't . . . I can't see that it
             works with cigarettes. I can with chocolate. It's
             right there.

Richard   What's the difference?

Eileen   I can't smell it, I can't taste it.

Richard   Yes, but you're not the one that's going to quit
             smoking.

Eileen   I need to know what it's like.

Richard   You don't have to feel it. I don't know what your
             habit is like. You know what any habit is like.
             That allows you to feel it enough (in fact maybe
             too much).

Eileen   Are you saying this works for whatever undesir-
             able thing you want to get rid of?

Richard   No, just compulsions that are unwanted not hem-
             orrhoids. More importantly you see, the nicest
             part about this process is we didn't have to make
             chocolate taste shitty, we don't have to make cig-
             arettes taste bad. The nice thing about here is I
             find that people who go around and help
             somebody quit smoking end up making assholes.
             They end up making assholes who go around tor-
             turing everybody in the world who still smokes.

Eileen   You mean the people who quit smoking?

Richard   Yes. They get these people to quit smoking, and
             then they go around and act like jerks. People
             who quit smoking end up like Christians, knock-
             ing on your door, harassing you at airports.
             Certain Christians in California think that every-
             body has to be a Christian. Want it or not. You
             go up to a Jew's door and tell him Jesus died for
             his sins. They go, "Oh yeah, let me tell you
             something, not for my sins he didn't. He died for
             your sins, not for mine, and he didn't knock on
             doors and pester anybody." This is the point in
             this example. She didn't have to make chocolate
             taste bad. She didn't have to criticize herself. She
             just used the natural method *the* brain learns with.
             You can develop a habit, too. This will work the
             other way around. The same mechanism can get
             you to crave and desire to do things. Like study.
             There are a lot of things that you want to do, and
             once you start doing them you're fine, it's just
             getting into the activity of doing it. You can make
             them compulsions. In essence I just simply traded
             one compulsion for another. One compulsion is
             the desire and craving for looking good, sounding
             good and feeling good in exchange for the desire
             for chocolate. In essence the mechanisms are not
             something that *I did to her.* I just told her what to
             do with her brain to get her in control of how it's
             done in the mind anyway. This is in essence a
             strategy. She has a strategy to end up with the
             desire of chocolate. Five times is not a lot, just
             because it's taken a whole lot of time here. Try

again. Go ahead and make a nice big bright picture of chocolate.

Eileen   I can't. And I'm really looking for . . .

Richard   Look at her. If you watch her face she'll go right into the second one. This doesn't seem to bother you a lot. So what happens is she says it had nothing to do with eating chocolate. It had to do with craving. It's not that she'll look at chocolate now on the outside and not have a choice. It's that what happens is . . . when she makes the picture in mind that created her desire for chocolate it simply now will propel her into another state where she really is more concerned with something else. And that's like eating mud. Who wants to eat mud? Only children, worms, and some people that I know who have awfully strange diets in California. There are people there who eat dirt. It's so organic. You can sell anything there that's organic. I was thinking of selling organic waste as a sure thing you could eat. Put a little stand up next to a sewer plant. I'm sure you could get people there to buy it.

Group   This seems like a thing we could use on our own without another person that would work just as well.

Richard   You could. She did it. I didn't do anything.

Group   She wouldn't have done it if you hadn't been there.

Richard   No, but she could have . . . once you know how
to do it. For example, it's always easier to have
somebody do something with you, since you can
follow instructions better that way. The thing
is . . . is that I have a better distinction of how
not to . . . you listen to the language, the
language will say, "I don't want this. I'm avoiding
that." And if you think about it, the things that
she's avoiding are . . . I don't want to have this
desire. She wants to avoid the desire, she can't
even avoid the chocolate. But the thing that you
are attracted to is much stronger than what you're
repelled away from. Think about being a
teenager. You have ample evidence of things that
you are afraid of. Even as an adult there's that
phenomenon where you're really attracted to
something that's not nearly as powerful as things
that you're really trying to avoid. You can get
people very easy . . . people get pulled into doing
things much more powerfully by being attracted
to them than being repulsed from them. There's
an old story that Dave Coloff told me. Funny, he
didn't cough at all yesterday. I think he should go
have a cocktail. Dave Coloff used to hypnotize
people and make cigarettes taste like something
horrible. Well, David Coloff considered the all-
time powerful thing of the century to be cod liver
oil. So David took this person who wanted to quit
smoking and hypnotized him . . . "cigarettes will
taste like cod liver oil." Sure enough the person
came back a month later. Dave said, "How's the
smoking?" The person said, "I don't smoke at
all." And David said, "No problem?" The guy

said, "No problem." While he was talking he opened his coat, pulled out a bottle of cod liver oil, and drank it. (Laughter) The thing is, whenever you do a substitution, funny things like that are going to happen. The choice that I made— about making what it is that you're attracted to looking, sounding and feeling good—is a choice in that I don't believe that you need to replace one compulsion with another, in terms of an object in the world. It's not a necessary thing. The actual compulsion is something that occurs in your mind. And that process needs to be turned into something else. This way the images of chocolate may come into her mind. They're only going to be there that long. And now her mind has learned what to do with them. I don't think you *do* things to people. I think you teach them. I know how to instruct someone in how to do this. If you go back through steps . . .

Eileen   Do you actually use this . . .

Richard   For myself?

Eileen   For yourself or anyone . . .

Richard   I don't want to quit though. It works too well.

Eileen   Could you use it for yourself if you wanted to?

Richard   Yes, ask Matt, he was there. Uh . . . it's much more elegant of a demonstration as far as I'm concerned if somebody else is here and does it to you than if I do it. Nothing in the world will get you

to stop. Believe me. You're all going to do this.
There's one thing I want to say about smoking is
that . . . the way in which I did it was, I made the
pleasure, interestingly enough, something that she
mentioned on her own. I got it so that what she
enjoyed was watching other people smoke.

Eileen   I've done that . . .

Richard   Obviously not very well. It's one thing to enjoy
watching other people smoke. It's another to
every time you want to smoke, have to shift to
that. The nice thing about this particular person
who quit, is not only did he quit smoking but he
didn't begin something that he likes. And they
also . . . because people who quit smoking, who
still have the compulsion left, can't afford for the
rest of the world to smoke. So the only thing
that's left to do is to get sick when they smell cig-
arette smoke. Become nauseous. It's going to be a
while (for her) . . . they have to go around acting
funny. I've been in rooms with ceilings eighty feet
high. There was one person smoking, and 200
yards away somebody else is raising his hand . . .
"Would you get that person to stop smoking?"—
me, I go lock that person in the closet with five
cigars. It is just a visual phenomenon . . . so to
me, it was always a very elegant thing, because
what happened was she enjoyed other people
smoking. As a transition, what happens is it then
becomes self-reinforcing—the more you don't
smoke the more you don't smoke. That's the
whole trick to making systems work. See, people
in psychotherapy, and everything now, the big

word is systems. Has been for ten years now.
Unfortunately they don't know what one is.
These family therapists, their idea of a system is
. . . they can use the word "process" now in place
of system. A system, especially a cybernetics one,
as it turns out, recently beyond cybernetics now.
In high-tech we discovered cybsystems aren't
where it's at. There are other kinds of systems
which are much more elegant in the way in
which they function. The people in communica-
tions have helping words. It's like feedback, feedforward. Feedback is good. Feedforward is bad.
And it turns out that this is the feedforward loop.
A self-reinforcing thing that turns something off is
of course something new. It's not a feedback.
Feedback loops are ones that will run on forever
the same way. People, they want to add feedback
into systems. They have open systems and closed
systems. If you read all the family therapy books,
you'd understand why I'm going, "God, if they
only knew what a system was." I mean . . . It was
a . . . behave yourself. Learn to be prepared.
(That, when I talk to you, some family therapy
groups say how can you treat individuals.) Your
book emphasizes . . . J. Haley, who by the way,
was the first person to review *The Structure of
Magic* before it ever came out, was sent the first
four chapters of the book. His response was that
people wouldn't find this interesting, that this is
old and obviously the people don't understand the
basics. They don't realize that putting the emphasis on the individual and not on the interaction of
the family, just like the old stuff in the twenties.

He told the publisher he shouldn't publish it. Stuff
like that. And from his point of view, that's probably accurate. There was old stuff from the twenties we were interested in getting published. But
the emphasis upon the individual is needed
because I think you should know how a family
system works as a family therapist. You should be
able to take any member in a family and shift the
whole system. It doesn't really matter which one
you get. Whether it's the identified client or not.
It could be just about any one, if you understand
how a system works. You can just take one of
them and go *pshhh* and tilt the system. So that the
system would change to the other. You can't do
that with one of them in the hospital. You need
to have the person interacting with a member of
the system. To me, that's what a family therapist
should be working towards. And you do that by
building a feedforward loop. Now I'll show you
what it is that I want you to do. The emphasis
that I talked about the first day was that to me,
NLP is an attitude and a methodology. Having an
attitude and methodology you can make up a
technique like that (fingers snap). How long
would it take . . . how many of you ever learned
to reframe, for example? Now out of those of you
who learned reframing, how long would it take to
do that with reframing?

Eileen   Oh, three times as long.

Richard   It would take at least three times as long, and
           that's if you're good at it. If you're good at it you
           can do it . . . it would take three times as long. If

you're not very good at it you can do it, but it might take you anywhere up to forever. This is pretty much the same way. If you're really not very good at it, it will still take you forever. If you're good at it, you can do it faster. As far as I'm concerned being good at it is being able to make up one. And this is really an opportunity, especially at this level of technology where instead of, like reframing, where there's a rote set of things that you go through, rather than using the same pattern, if you think about being able to intensify and diminish the intensity of feelings and other things. What happens when you turn the sound up, sound down, this and that? You talk about compulsions, strong desire, strong feelings. Well, here's an easy way to control that compulsion. To direct somebody towards something. The nice effect that this has, is that what it is she would become more compulsive about is the thing that you want. It doesn't just emphasize getting rid of the desire for chocolate. She now is going to be stuck with viewing it right, and it's going to be powerful. See . . . for example, is there anything that you do that is something that you do to improve the way that you look and feel? Do you occasionally do any such activities?

Eileen   Hatha yoga.

Richard   Yoga. Are you compulsive about doing it?

Eileen   No.

Richard	Well, think about doing yoga. When you think about doing it, what happens?
Eileen	I get very relaxed.
Richard	When you think about sitting down and doing yoga . . .
Eileen	Lying down.
Richard	Pardon? (Lifts hand to ear)
Eileen	Lying down.
Richard	Okay. When you think about it (yoga) in the past, sitting down and actually doing it, you go do it?
Eileen	Not always.
Richard	When was the last time you did it?
Eileen	A couple of months ago?
Richard	When do you think the next time you do it will be? (laughing)
Eileen	(Group laughter) (laughing) Probably tonight.
Richard	Could be. (Turns to group) How many times do you think she'll do it between now and the next time you guys meet as a group? (one month) More than once? Well eventually it will be more than it was last month. And it won't be a struggle. (Pause) I believe that anything that you have to struggle to do is based on not having yourself organized internally in advance. The technology

to make your brain prepared to learn or do with ease has never existed. Now, it's not, and I *emphasize this, not* that I want you to go through and do exactly what I did with Eileen. *I want you* to think about when I talked about having extensive exploration, and say, let's take Eileen for example. Do I know people who work with . . . you are now. Sit down with this person here. (Laughter) . . . so literal, you are so literal.

Eileen   Like a trained seal.

Richard   It certainly is. (Imitates her eye movements) Anyway, you had said something about having bet whether you would be able to induce someone into quitting smoking. Well, if you sit down you can find out whether or not you can. Like you said, you couldn't see in your mind and understand how chocolate and cigarettes could be the same. But we're not talking about something so literal here. We're talking about the land of concepts, and this particular thing is where there are all these different pieces. We know that in order for somebody to have a compulsive behavior . . . before we end up with behavior we have to have something behind it. Right, a brain and all those weird things that it does. We also know that theoretically we have somebody else's brain in there thinking on it. So we have individual parameters. Did they give a list of some submodalities?

Eileen   We made our own list.

Richard   You made your own list. I'll try to listen to this
               group. But anyway, you all ended up knowing
               that there is more contrast, color, size . . .

Group   Distance . . .

Richard   Now, the parameters that I used were, of course,
               brightness and size. Okay . . . now we know that
               again, statistically . . . did you guys get some syn-
               thetic ones? I use these two to control intensity
               and something else . . . direction of that to . . . or
               what we might refer to as contact. See, the bright-
               ness factor is capable of controlling the intensity. I
               used size to get it to switch and to go in a new
               direction. That's why you have to use more than
               one parameter to get the change from one thing
               to something else.

Eileen   You mean size to . . . repeat that again?

Richard   In other words, I use brightness to control the
               strength of a feeling. And I've used the size to do
               the same thing. Right. In other words, there are
               two images. You feel them pull this way, but if
               this one gets darker, this one gets bigger. You
               change the direction of where the behavior is
               aimed for. Now, I could have used distance. You
               could have had one get bigger and move away
               while the other one came closer. There's lots of
               choices about how to do this. It's not that one
               works and one doesn't. Just as long as you keep in
               mind that you're doing two things. You're not
               just making feelings diminish. You want them to
               do it by themselves. So that when they're out,

once you get out there in the world, the desire hits, it goes . . . *shoooo* into something else. Changes into a new direction. It's like when you know you're walking in and you're really going to do something. Really got yourself wound up, step in there and *whoooo* do a new thing instead of the same old thing you always do. Do you know what I'm talking about? Well that's where you do this all by yourself. Now you have a chance to change those too. Now the trick is to go through the following steps. The first one is caliber. This means . . . you've got to know what the chocolate one looks like. Here's a big brown chocolate image there. She had that look on her face? Okay. Then I've got to compare that with the look on her face about something that feels good, which is the image of her looking good and feeling good, and not the image of her being sick, but the image of her feeling good and looking good, so that I have stage one and stage two. What I'm attempting to do now is change from stage one to stage two automatically, so that I can get her feedback. So the first thing is to know which one is which, so that you can tell whether or not it's working when you have them run through it five times. The second thing is to arrange a system. The system in this case is: I know how to turn down the intensity of something, to get it to be possible for something else to get in. Now, not only am I going to need to turn it down, I'm going to need to be able to have the other one available to step in. So that's where it's going to introduce a new element. The system is . . . is one of arranging. So

what you're going to have to do is decide first
how to control two variables. And the variables,
of course, are going to be intensity and content.
Then you simply assign what works, and in this
case, that is . . . in most of the cases in here
you've already explored with people. Now, with
some people you have to remember—if you
intensify the brightness the feelings get weaker. So
the calibration stage is one where you also have
got to figure that out. Do you remember that
from that exercise? Okay. We went through this
this morning. Fresh in your mind. The system is
where you've also then got to find one more.

"The system is. . ."

This refers to something we discussed earlier in the seminar.

*When you work with a system you have to find at least one
more element to be able to move the content. When people
tell you, for example, that their experience is "see elevator—
be afraid," there has to be at least one more element involved
before you have the basis for a change, and at least part of
that element has to be unconscious. You have to find one
more submodality, one more step in the strategy, one more
phenomenon.*

Whenever you're going to change content, think
about what changes content. The thing is that
memories could fade. Listen to the things you've
heard people say. Memories fade . . . they get
smaller. Instead of using size, I could have had an
image get darker, reach blur, have the other one
blur back in. All of those things . . . just think
about going to the movies. The only one that
doesn't work good is jumping. You know where

you flash from one scene to another, you're
always going, "Is this a flashback, or what is this?"
You want the nice ones when they blur. The nice
thing about size is that proportional change allows
them to be able to do it on their own. You don't
have to go, now you introduce the new one. You
have a vote . . . there to kind of work with anyway. You can use . . . oh you can do all kinds of
geometric wonders with them. Now, the third
key that you want to be able to do is to automate.
She told a lie back there. She said she wanted to
be in control. That's bullshit. She just doesn't like
the way she's out of control. She's just out of control now. She's just in control of the way she
wants to be. It's more pleasant to her. Nobody
wants to be in control because then you have to
make decisions constantly, every moment of your
life. "Breathe, now breathe out, oops, should I
beat the heart?" . . . You don't want that kind of
control. Being in control, to me . . . Who needs
it, right? And then if you don't like the way it is,
then you can break in and change the whole trip.
This system now will compel her more and more
to do things. Make her feel better, make her look
better. Now at some point in time that may,
because it's going to be automated, it's going to
run off just like the chocolate thing did. Now the
thing is, at some point in time it may run into a
snag, or what in our profession we refer to as a
bug. When it does, then you account for that at
that time. You are never going to be able to find
something that's entirely predictable in nature.
But you always attempt to find something where

a system will run by itself, to the best of your ability to predict, in the way that they are efficient.
Imagine if you gave her an aversion to chocolate.
Well, then she has to give up eating . . . and
enjoying it, and then, of course you'll probably
camp on her children for eating it. And when
other people are sitting at the dinner table and
they start to eat it, you go *blaaaahh* . . lose friends
. . . people will say, "she's grumpy" . . .
Hundreds of people will lose their jobs. We don't
want that kind of reverberation going around.
Now she'll just be a self-serving, glamorous person. Her husband will go, "Will you stop doing
all this? I don't like looking at you." She'll get in
fights with people. They'll get divorced, ruin their
children's lives, and all end up in psychoanalysis.
But anyway, the thing is, to me, the most important part of this is that second stage, that when
you pick one with what we're dealing with here
is, to me, the most important part of this is that
second stage, that when you pick one with what
we're dealing with here is that it's all pleasant. I
want you to think about that. There ain't no shit
in this at all. Now there are ways of dealing with
unpleasant stuff like, for example, you can cure
phobias with this. Can you imagine a faster way of
curing a phobia than a phobia cure? How many of
you know that standard phobia thing? A standard
phobia cure takes about ten minutes. Or you can
do it with this one in about three minutes. Why
should you take ten whole minutes to do it?
(Laughter)

Group	But we get paid; how will we make a living?
Richard	Not if you're smart you won't! You can always get people to enjoy taking enough time to make your car payment. Right now, people are locked into the thing that the amount of what you get is based on the number of hours. Not even minutes you sit with them. I was speaking of clients, not you. (Referring to expert member of group) The thing is that people require . . . the truth of the matter is, it's not the number of hours, it's the amount of possibilities to get people there, and the thing is . . . is that for me, like in my teaching I cease to worry about whether or not something is the case. If I find that I have hours of materials . . . then will it actually get done? Chances are that I won't have the patience to lay down the groundwork rotely enough to teach you how to really use what I teach exquisitely. My peers have gotten to the point now where they're almost afraid to send me alone, when I'll just go out and have a good time. Alright people, here we are, let's party. So you can sit down and talk to somebody and compute what the best way to do it with them is. Which is ultimately what we have been trying to work towards for years, is a way to sit down, do a few things with somebody and to be able to calculate the most efficient system of what to use with them. Just say, "Hey you, hey . . . go home and do yoga." (Laughter) Yes, yes, I know you were listening.
Eileen	Can I go home now? (Laughter)

Richard   Compulsions have their ways.

Group   How would you deal with phobia? What are they first?

Richard   How would you deal with phobia? What is a phobia?

Group   Most of them are fears.

Richard   That's what it is. Does anyone here have a phobia? Alright. She has a phobia. Fix her phobia for her. Now how do you proceed? I'll tell you exactly. Automate it where you take your fear, take it to pieces. Have somebody do it five times. That will automate it. Then you stop and you check it again and see if it works, and if you watch her each of those five times she went through stage one and stage two. Each time she did it, it went faster and then at the end I had to go in and do it and it went *whooooosh*. So it's automatic.

Group   Is there something to do for her to reinforce that later . . . that automation?

Richard   Let her try and get out of it, to tell you the truth. Let her try and have a desire for chocolate.

Eileen   How can I have a desire for chocolate when I can't picture it, smell it?

Richard   Well, you could picture and smell it. She pictured it and smelled it before.

Eileen   I can't now.

Richard   You're going to have to have some first. She's
              saying, "How do you do this?" You people sat in
              here, man, and you didn't hear that. Because she
              cried and wailed and beat up some chair you'd be
              depressed. But this fucking human sits in there
              and goes, "This desire overwhelms me. How can
              I have a fucking desire?" (Laughter) You should
              be going, "Hey man, I don't have to have my
              clients act like jerks in order to change. You
              know, you don't have to go and spill your guts.
              You don't have to cry and moan. You go *swish*
              and change is there." That's technology. This
              means you don't have to (hit, hit, hit), you just
              have to go *whooooooo*, (imitating client). I wonder
              what I can get from that. I don't want you to be
              impressed with me, I want you to go greed . . .
              (makes face)

Eileen   I'm impressed with the process.

Richard   Good. Do you know what being impressed is?
              Being impressed is where your hands don't have
              to come together, and you go in to thoughts like
              "What can I get for myself?" *Greed*. This is what I
              want. I want people who go inside and go, "I can
              get my weight where I want it without having to
              work, I can get myself to study and enjoy the hell
              out of it." What can I do? Where's the limits?
              Because you're about to get one choice. Not only
              are you going to get one choice you may go
              spread this around to your clients. This is right.
              You can wipe out your practice with this. Or you

can really turn it into something where you work
for two hours a week and get paid the same. You
will not want for referrals if you succeed. And if
you tell people that you don't usually see people
for very long, and that you charge by the change
from the initial meeting, you make a deal and you
give it to them and you take their money and be
surprised. I always used to start my business by
asking people, "How much have you spent on
this so far?" (Laughter) I'm serious. You're dealing
with a phobia, man. You'll find out. They go, "I
don't know." I go, "Figure it out." I have people
who've spent $16,000 to $30,000 trying to change
one thing. Think about that. Thirty thousand for
one lousy phobia! I had one guy who spent
$30,000 to get rid of one phobia, and $105 when
he came to me. They generalized it (Laughter).
The guy comes in and all he's got is one lousy
phobia. And the guy tried to help him. Do you
know what he does? Now think about your phobia. And the guy goes *Ohhhhhhh*. Now think of
something in your personal life that makes you
feel secure. You know, like your home. The guy
couldn't go home, he was afraid of his ex-wife,
terrified of his children. I mean the guy's life got
ruined by this person. The psychiatrist reassured
him he was on the edge of that anyway. Border-
line, you know. (Laughter) Oh, you should see
what I did to the shrink too. (Laughter). I paid
him back in full. I said, "Well, let me show you
something. Is there anything in your life that ter-
rifies you? I mean something that scares the shit
out of you? That you're really REALLY afraid of?

Answer that and sit down." (Laughter). I believe
that people usually get what they deserve. Some
people get away with a little bit here and there.
And every once in a while, people really get their
just rewards, so to speak. Things have a way of
coming around again; sometimes it takes longer
than we would like it to, but it happens. I have a
friend who ended up getting elected to a political
office. I could think of nothing worse to happen
to the guy, who was a rad when I was in college.
He had to go off to Sacramento, California to be a
State Legislator. Of course I went in and said
"You're not going to take all that money. You're
always bitching at everyone else. You wouldn't
do that would you?" Then I started a movement
to have him recalled. Eventually it had an interesting effect. He discovered . . . and went back and
apologized to all the politicians he used to pick
on. I thought he was very unkind to them. How
can you criticize somebody for doing something
until you know what it's about? It's a little like
saying, "Here, take these drugs." I say to the
schoolteacher, "No, you take them." And they
say, "No, they're harmful. But not to children." I
don't approve of that attitude. Me, I'd take them
and find out what happens for a while first. No,
it's not harmful, it makes the old ladies bald.
Now, what is a phobia? You tell people you have
a phobia. What are you phobic about?

Fear of Worms

Richard   What are you phobic about?

Anita   Worms.

Richard   Worms. Take a picture of worms. Oh there,
          we've got one. *Yaaaahhh.*

Group   *Ohhhhhhheeeeeeee.*

Richard   We can get into this. Before the phobia gets away,
          you anchor it. And you think about not paying.
          You always want to say that at the end. I get these
          people and they go, "That was too fast, I'm not
          going to pay you your $5,000," and I go *"quish"*
          and they say, "Well, maybe I will." Because with
          skill you could always make a fear of walking out
          of the office door, wearing clothes . . . anything.
          So, here. All it takes is a picture of worms. Here
          we have a picture with worms in it. You look at
          the picture of worms. (Laughter) They're not
          even worms. (Laughter) Crawling all over the
          place. Does it have to be that picture? Bigger than
          the one by your foot?

"Bigger than the one . . . "

I look down at her foot and she jumps out of her chair. She
didn't have to do anything; she was four feet in the air,
which tells me her feeling is automated. When clients have
to stop and think about it, you can be pretty sure that
you're dealing with a fear. (See p. ?? of Chapter 1,
"Anticipatory Loss.")

Anita   Any kind of worm. I usually go *yeech.*

Richard   Like the one by your feet, you mean?

Anita   My head.

Richard   Oh just the ones in your head. These don't count, right. They're just lines on paper. They're not worms. We can have a new movie, *Attack of the Killer Worms*. Did you ever see *Attack of the Killer Tomatoes?*

Anita   No.

Richard   If you ever get a chance, see that movie. That was nominated the worst film ever made. And literally, these giant tomatoes roll down the street and crush people. But now we have a new one. Now, what's the difference between this . . . we now have a compulsion causes a void. Now, what do we want to do? See where we're going. This is stage one. We want to go to stage two. What is stage two? We don't want her to fall in *love* with worms. (Laughter) We can, though. Imagine that she can be a fisherman for a living. Would you like to be able to put a worm on a hook? Go fishing?

Anita   I'd like to be able to pick one up in the garden. I cannot touch worms. I stand in front . . . when I get that close I can't put my fingers on one. I can pick them up with gloves on.

Richard   You can stand to look at them?

Anita   Oh I can look at them. I'm afraid . . . if somebody in this room had a worm . . .

Richard   How about snakes?

Anita   I'm easier with snakes.

Richard   You can pick up snakes?

Anita   Well I've never had to pick up a snake. I'd rather
               pick up a snake than a worm. If I had a choice.

Richard   I have a snake that lives in my house. The most
               disgusting thing that you could find. Brings all
               these things home. The snake gets out and wraps
               around the lamp, people come over and turn the
               lamp on . . . you should see the look on their
               faces. (Laughter) We let it run around the house.
               If you want to see a surprised look on people's
               faces . . . "Come on over, have a couple of cock-
               tails." They will sit down and be sitting there
               when this thing rounds the corner. At first their
               eyes won't even accept the visual input. It keeps
               coming and coming and coming. And it has a way
               of sort of moving around the lamps and furniture
               and branches and stuff for it. They go, "Oh, oh,
               oh, oh." They usually say, "Oh don't worry about
               Alex. Alex won't bother you." The snake has an
               attraction to new people. Slithers around and of
               course, you try and act cool. Then you look and
               the snake's nine feet long and headed straight
               toward you. Snakes are cold blooded, so they like
               to wrap around you to keep warm. A nine-foot
               boa constrictor . . . if you never held a snake, his
               whole goal in life while you're there is to wrap
               around you to stay warm. Then they nod out and
               that's a good thing. You go in the bathroom and
               open the shower, and there's this nine-foot boa
               constrictor hanging from the faucet. It sort of
               gives you a start in the morning.

Anita   No, I don't want to run across snakes.

Richard   But we're doing an NLP testing this year in New
               Wave. Have you seen *Raiders of the Lost Ark?*
               (Laughter) I love it when he looks down and
               goes, "It had to be snakes!" Now with her it will
               be, "It had to be worms!" Okay now, where are
               we going to? What happens when we have her
               make a picture of worms? This is something
               where, when she sees it, do you get body
               tremors? When that same picture occurs, what do
               we want there? This one goes into fear. So how
               about . . . we want her to go into okay. How
               about curiosity? Let's give it a little juice. There
               are already enough people in the world who feel
               okay. I'm tired of that word. It's just not a
               descriptive word. Okay is a concept. We could
               even go with so what. Anything but okay. I'm
               tired of asking people how they feel and have
               them say okay. How about not bad. You don't
               want to go around and wipe out all the feelings
               people have. How about if we go for curiosity?
               We could go for hunger. (Laughter) You can
               make it anything you want to have. Just make
               sure it's an existing state. You can be curious. She
               says when she's out in the garden . . . when
               you're out in the garden it tells you something.
               It's either, she's out there because she's depressed
               and she wants to eat the worms, or she is going
               out to the garden to do some gardening. I go out
               and buy worms to put in my garden. Spread them
               around, chop them up to make more. You chop
               them in half and they make two worms. That's

how you grow worms. You could have your own worm farm. When she comes back out eating worm sandwiches, look out. You ask her, as part of this thing here . . . calibrating is that you want to find out what state is she going to go into. Never accept a non-powerful state, because if you're going from fear to something, going from fear to nothing . . . it's not that groovy. If you're going to go from fear to nothing, we have a different way of going about that. When you want to end up with really dull people we have a model for that. Here are the transitions, right. Well, now all you need is which parameters you're going to operate.

Anita   Would you get what you want?

Richard   He's going to do this. We're each going to do our own. I'm just trying to give you a demonstration.

Group   The fact that avoidance is there really has nothing to do with self . . .

"The fact that avoidance. . ."

This is an elegant demonstration of how most clinicians think.

A lot of people who have matching strategies think learning is finding things that match what they already know. That's exactly the opposite of real learning. That's actually distorting everything so it fits what you already understand. This is one of the problems with clinical education—it teaches people to diagnose for meaning. They have categories and look for things that fit into the categories. If it fits into the category then they've learned it. This is a real indication that you

have a deductive thinker, and what you have to do is go back
and make categories like "new." Now find something that
fits into that.

Richard   Alright. This is a compulsion. The only difference
                 is that we're dealing with something that's being
                 avoided. What are we going to do? We're going
                 to decrease her fear. We water it down, dilute it,
                 and we then stick in something else. This has got
                 to be turned down, and then she turns up some-
                 thing else . . . curiosity, humor, being amused. If
                 you decrease it then it will go back. Did you ever
                 spend . . . in school? Okay, never mind. Just
                 dilute it down . . .

When I say to "just dilute it down," I'm responding to
what I see. I can tell what she's doing visually, and this is
not discernible from the transcript.

The trick in working with submodalities is to realize the
function of the submodalities themselves. When you turn
the brightness down the intensity of feelings decreases
almost proportionally. Submodalities are nonlinear
variables, but they function almost linearly. So when you
want to turn down the intensity of a feeling by turning the
brightness down, submodalities allow you to turn another
feeling up; basically, that's how you learn to trade one feeling for another. You go, "Not this, THIS." Not craving
chocolate—being in control of yourself. You can literally
shift one desire or feeling for another by controlling the
simultaneity of the images themselves.

The basic trick I'm trying to get across to the group is that
you can control your brain by learning how to use the differences in analog variables. Whenever it happened in the
past, the synapses fired off automatically and gave the person a predictable feeling. But if you train people to turn the
brightness or the size down as soon as the image is there,

the brain goes, "Diminish those feelings!" The brain doesn't care whether it is a craving for chocolate, a fear of flying, or any positive or negative feeling; it doesn't make those distinctions. It only makes the distinction between "intensify—diminish."

Another approach uses threshold patterns. In threshold patterns you literally take a feeling or a fear through the ceiling and blow it out, as I did in the case of the "chocolate lady." This comes from the same model that is used in bending sheet metal. You bend it suddenly and quickly with more thrust than it can possibly stand and it changes form. Well, the mathematics of catastrophe theory was developed by the human brain; that's why we understand it and so it works for the human brain as well.

By the same token, decreasing the intensity of an undesirable feeling and bringing up the intensity of a desired state is something the brain understands—"It's not that, it's THIS." The brain itself works very simply. It's a binary machine; that's why all our mathematics are binary. It's trinary capabilities are not for most people—yet. That's why most people don't understand holograms.

you don't have to go all the way down to nothing. Leave it down until the other one shoots up. In other words, whatever you desire, something that feels good, you're going to be attracted to. Whatever is the good feeling is going to work. It's not going to be able to overcome the fear, it will dilute it until it can go up by itself. She will have to turn it down, just like this person turns down one and increases the other. There's a point at which it goes *WHAP* and that's why she's going to make the picture now. When you dilute a feeling, you find one that's there. It doesn't have to be related either.

"It doesn't have to be related either."

You can think of the brain as a three-dimensional matrix. The neurocortical pathways can go in multiple directions, which is why people respond one way in one situation and in a different way in another situation. Basically what I did with Anita was set up a matrix that would determine pathways for her. As long as she accesses her history one way she would continue the same behavior. But if I set up a different matrix she will only access different parts of her history in that context, which will produce new behavior in the future.

The elements of the matrices have to do with the way people are doing transderivational search through time into their histories. The notion of timelines is probably one of the most misunderstood ideas in NLP. A lot of NLP practitioners believe there is a timeline. There isn't one timeline but a series of them, and they have to do with the way people access history.

Take a depressive. Depressives actually have fun, but when they look back they'll always say the same thing: "Well, at the time I thought I was having fun, but when I think about it now I really wasn't." They literally go back and change history and don't reaccess the positive feelings.

When people go into the future with fear it's based on having had fear, but fear isn't universally true across their experience. Even if they say they're afraid of elevators there are situations where they have been in, on, around or near elevators but knew they weren't getting on one. They have a whole other history where they've had different reactions to them.

So if you set up a matrix that allows them to access only these memories, or doesn't allow them to access anything about elevators, but enables them to access things that changed—the kind of history on which basis they can generate new behavior—they end up with a new branch in their future timeline.

Whatever the cure . . . In her case this is really
double play,

"Double play. . ."

When you do a swish pattern it's really important to associate people with their problems. If the problem is chocolate or worms or Ferraris or beautiful women—whatever their compulsion is—you always start by having them see just the object. And then you swish it to where they see themselves with control over it.

It's a double play. You're swishing from direct experience to indirect experience because people are never going to walk outside and see themselves. The only place you see yourself is in the mirror or in "your own" movie. What you're doing is getting them to pay attention to whatever the external stimulus is and then to go inside their heads so they have control. If the outside experience controls them, you go inside; if the inside experience controls them, you go outside. It's that simple.

because she does want to feel but she can't. Then you have to go for a positive example of that which is she really sees herself as being a more competent person and if she could do this would be an example of something.

Anita   It's such a dumb thing.

Richard   Alright . . . and you see yourself as a much better person. That positive thing will clamp right in when you resolve your fear. You put one in the corner, right, one up here, and then *shooo* it will go. The only thing you have to do is check to make sure that . . . how size operates and brightness operates. Because if you have on the opposite way, then it would come out. Some people, the bigger the picture the less it affects them too. So you can't just count on it to have an effect. If you take a picture and have them make it smaller and then bigger and find out what happens. This is the game where you go in and play, and find your own way to do it. Whichever is more powerful will work. All you do is dilute what is not wanted and intensify what is wanted. Put them in a relationship to one another so that when you get to a certain point it will snap, and the other one goes in. And it's there. And you can see it and you go *waaaaah*. And you watch them. You can't get the picture of the worms up there by themselves. Then, of course, you need another piece. What you do is . . . you have to find out, do you put it far away?

"What you do IS . . . you have to find out"

The tonal punctuation is the critical part here. It's in essence a verbal swish pattern. Most of the time I do that with scope ambiguity. "You have a terrible problem and everybody already knows . . . it . . . doesn't really matter."

So you can bring it up again until you can get it close enough? You may have to play around a little with it.

Group   I have a question. This one is different because there you're dealing with the images, but how about when she gets there and sees the actual worm, like in the other case the actual chocolate? Eileen is going to see the chocolate and still want it and be able to eat it.

Richard   No, she's not going to want it when she sees it.
               When she sees it she'll be able to decide whether
               she wants it or not. She'll have a choice. Yes, but
               where do you make choices? Good thinking.

Anita   The one desired state for me would be to go out
               there and see the worm and look at that thing,
               well . . .

Richard   No, no, no, no, no. See, you're stuck in content
               here.

This is a tonal step down, with the stress on "here." She's
focusing on the worms; by focusing on what's in an image
rather than on its form, she's at the mercy of the content
because she can't alter the form.

So when she says, "The one desired state for me would be
to go out there and see the worm and look at that thing,
well. . .", I interrupt her to say, "No, no, no, no, no. See
you're stuck in content here." ("Here" implies not in other
places.)

By interrupting her I make sure that, instead of focusing on
what used to be the problem, she focuses on a new direction. The rule of thumb in NLP is that if you're looking
for problems, you'll find them; if you're looking for things
to avoid, you'll find them; if you're looking for what you
can control, you'll find that. That's the shift I'm trying to
make in her.

All these clients have one thing in common: to me, their
problems are trivial. I know I can make quick changes that
would not last, but there's no point in doing that unless I
can do it so they begin to live more generatively. I use
change work to move people in a direction that enables
them to begin to take control over their minds. And that is
still just an example of what I want them to do with a lot

of things. It's the difference between looking for an
outcome and looking for a direction.

You've got to watch out for content. It's going to
get you some day. I know, I know. I remember
the conversation with that. It doesn't even have to
be about worms. There's something that's much
more important than worms to her. It's some
thing so stupid. It's like a counter-example to the
way she thinks of herself as being a competent
human being. If she can go out and do this, it will
be an example to her of something that she really
wants. Just the same way *not* having the desire
about chocolate will be an example to her of the
kind of thing that personal confidence in her case,
the inverse of the fact of having ugly skin and not
being in control of your experience. Now she can
have the other. It's an example that says, "Hey,
you can have it." That's what's attractive to you.
The worm is only a representation of that.

Anita   How about spaghetti?

Richard   Then you won't be able to touch spaghetti. *Yech.*
Me, I'm building a fear of. . . . find somebody in
here, and find some, for example, let's play . . . is
there anything else, see for him, (pointing to one
of the participants) he wants to know how to do
phobias. She wants to know how to do smoking.
Is there anybody in here who wants to learn how
to do something specific? Oh my God.

Group   I want to make money. Lots of money.

Richard   You have a phobia of making money?

Group   I think so.

Richard   Is there somebody who wants to deal with some-
             body who gets their own way about making
             money? Because I'm convinced that that's what
             most people's difficulty is with making it. I can't
             understand how people have trouble making
             money. It's utterly preposterous to me, because
             you can't come from any lower on the bottom
             than I did. Unless you came from some country in
             Africa. There are places in Africa where you can
             be poorer than I was. At least there was something
             around to steal where I was. If you grow up
             where everybody's poor, then there's nothing to
             steal. At least there were people around where I
             could slither up the neighborhood and break in
             somewhere or something. That's a little different,
             you can get poorer, but in the country where I
             grew up it's hard. You have to go way out in the
             hills or something, and then there's stuff laying
             around to eat. Coming from where I did it's hard
             for me to understand when people come in and
             tell me about how they can't make money. I'm
             usually going, "Hmmm, yes? well . . . And
             they're going, Well, . . . yeah." It's just like the
             people come in and they go . . . I go, "Well, why
             don't you go try . . ." and they go, "Well, I tried
             that." And so I think it's a legitimate request and
             that people, when they think about something
             duh, duh . . . "I need to make money . . . duh. I
             tried this one thing and it didn't work. I'd better
             try it again. I think about it but, you know . . .

going and doing it . . . I'd like to make some
money . . . I'd better stay where I am and not
think about anything. But I'd really like to make
money." I hear that shit all the time. It's no problem making money. You can get a shotgun and
make money. If you want to make money and
have a good time then you don't go study
psychology. You go and study economics. You
don't study in school, you go out and find people
who make money. You go, "How do you do
this?" and they'll tell you how, but never again.
Glue it on the mirror. They'll look you straight in
the eye and say, "Well, what have you got?" And
they'll go, "Well, why don't you do this?"
Inevitably somebody will go, "Wellllll yeah,
ohhhh." They never go, "Well, that's a good
idea. I'll take this here, but I don't know about
this here. So I'll go find someone who knows."
When I wanted to become a publisher, I just
went to a publisher and went, "Hey, how do you
do this?" He said, "You do this, this, this and
this." They don't even charge you. When I
wanted to do hypnosis I went to . . . I just want
to write a book about it and be an expert. This is
how you do it. Why mess around? You'd be surprised at these people in the phone book. You
say, "I hear you do this, and I want to do this, and
I'm going to and if it's not you it's someone else."
And they go, "Gosh, hey, sign me up." You'd be
surprised. The only time I ever had any difficulty
getting any help anywhere whatsoever was from
my advisor in college. That and from doctors in
the emergency ward. I've been in the emergecy

ward with my elbow sticking out here and my
arm twisted and broken for about three hours.
And they come and say, "Sign this." I love that.
"Just sign with your other hand." They do that
you know. And finally I went up and said, "Are
you a doctor?" "Yes." I walked up and I reached
over and grabbed him by the throat . . . put your
thumb up and grab a little nerve and I went, "See
this arm? It hurts. Do you know what pain is?"
He says, "It does look like it hurts. Why don't
you and I go in the other room? Let's go in the
other room." Then I gave up emergency wards. I
decided they didn't function well. Who wants to
help somebody overcome their money problems?
In this group you won't find anybody who hasn't
overcome them. Somebody is already doing
something with you. Maybe we could make
everything work out. I'm trying to find out if
somebody wants to. What did you want to do?
I was asking for people who wanted to do things,
not have it done to them. What do you want
to do?

Group	Weight . . .
Richard	Okay. Does somebody want to do weight? That's a standard. You could open up a weight clinic and make a mint. You ought to work with him and then you'll have no problem. You open a weight clinic that's successful five times, it will carry you for ten years.
Group	Appetite.

Richard   Appetite? You don't want to control your weight,
             just your appetite? I agree. They're different.
             Don't laugh. Somebody else wants to do weight?
             Appetite? Do you want to do appetite? Do his
             appetite. Somebody else . . . do we have weight
             back here? Who wants to do weight?

Group   How about waiting?

Richard   Is there anything else you guys would like to get
             together and find someplace to do it and go do it?
             What you've got here is a high-powered technol-
             ogy. Sounds like we have a small fear over here.
             Yes. But if you quit smoking how will it . . .
             would it allow you to dance? It was not a relevant
             content. It was . . . I mean why do you want to
             bother to quit? Do you see yourself looking better
             or feeling better? Move better, more freely. But
             you wouldn't have to dance day and night. This
             would wear you out. Why don't you go back on
             your own, and maybe change that one so that it
             doesn't exhaust you and you don't have to smoke
             cigarettes to relax? We had the right idea there,
             we just went overboard a little bit. Every once in
             a while we become overzealous here. Motivation
             is what we talked about. Her motivation is not to
             dance, but to feel better. So we want her to see an
             image of herself looking and feeling better, and all
             of those things. This is the kind of thing . . . if we
             have her image dancing her heart out, then after
             she does this for a while she'll get exhausted, and
             looking back maybe get a weak picture of a ciga-
             rette, but at least there's a place to rest. I did a
             thing in Philadelphia . . . No, I don't. No. She's

too young. Must be *Grimm's Fairy Tales*. Well, you know how that old German stuff . . . you know. I think that's where it came from. Just don't do that in surgery.

Group   While Eileen was doing it, I was sitting next to her. I found it amazing that, although Eileen was working with you, I could go along with what she was doing and feel it for myself.

Richard   This is really form. That's the difference between form and content. You don't have to have red shoes and tap dance either.

Group   I worked with Susan and her situation with such a strong phobic response that I couldn't really elicit any submodalities for her present state, because even the thought or the mention of the word . . . I could not . . .

Richard   What word?

Group   Praying mantis. She couldn't even look. She just had this overwhelming feeling. Finally got it down to a little dot two miles away, and she could deal with that. But every time I tried to bring it up . . .

Richard   You couldn't get it there?

Group   Well, no. What I had to do is . . . I had to do a disassociation. I had to have her float up and see herself sitting on the floor looking at this dot. And then I could bring it up.

Richard   Oh yes, then I told you that distance wasn't the
                 right one, position was. See, the phobia occurs as
                 part of this model. An example of it, and position
                 is not that phobia cures are different. It's only an
                 example. Positions in space are one of the
                 variables. So when you found out that distance
                 wasn't appropriate, then you used position instead
                 of distance.

What I'm trying to get across to these people is to pay
attention to which variables make a difference with which
people and when. It's important to focus on whether disassociation, position in space, the actual location of an image,
the distance or the brightness are the critical variables people can manipulate in their minds to produce lasting
change.

With Susan, distance was the critical variable; position
didn't make much difference. Using distance to alter position in space produced a much better outcome with her
than the inverse sequence. It's a question of which
submodalities you vary when.

Group   Then I could bring her closer, where she could
                 see it and then work with it.

Richard   It's just that distance wasn't a very good choice.
                 Size . . . the position in space really was . . .

Group   There are people who can't see their images.

Richard   It's not that they don't see them, it's that they
                 don't remember. What I've discovered through
                 the years is you ask the questions like, "What
                 color are your mother's eyes?" and they'll tell you.
                 I mean, the information is there; you just tell
                 them to pretend. Or you can show them . . .

usually the images are not what they think they are. You can take somebody who, quote, "Doesn't see images," and start asking them all these questions. Ask them, "What color are your mother's eyes?" they go, "Brown." How do you know that? That is the image. Typically if you don't make it into a life-and-death struggle, what they can't do is hold it still where they can look at them. The other thing is if the people who tell you they can't see images are, typically . . . they do see images, it's just that they don't know what they're seeing . . . see clouds. That's an image. Yeah, we could always get a little wind going and blow the clouds out of the way. In order to do it, they can tell you what's behind them. Talk to that person. They're there, and the thing is it's like the arm levitation. Don't make a life-and-death struggle out of it. Just go for it. There are lots of other parameters to work with. Typically if people can't see images it's just a way of stopping themselves from scaring themselves. A lot of it has to do with the fact that the intensity of feelings is so connected with images . . . that if you ask them and they tell you if you've started to see their images. Their feelings become so intense, it's frightening. What you need to do is find your way around that.

I encounter this all the time. The first thing I ask most people who don't see their images is what they do for a living. Then I'll ask them about their history; typically they have really gruesome stuff.

There was a pathologist in one seminar who worked in forensic medicine and had to cut up corpses all day. All of his pictures were about people who had been murdered. The people working in his group despaired of trying to get him to see other pictures. They didn't understand that it was not that he couldn't see his images; he couldn't see them the way they were asking him to. That's all there was to it.

If you asked him about his furniture he'd tell you what color it was. If you asked him whether he would like to rearrange his living room, he'd say "no." If you asked him how he had decided that, he'd tell you, "Well, those aren't real pictures." For him "real pictures" were connected with feelings that scared the hell out of him.

In this case we altered the pathologist's transderivational search for images and made him use a semantic prime that distinguished living and dead things, so when he accessed past pictures they were of living things, not dead and gruesome things.

The mind functions by amnesia; what you're not aware of constitutes the largest part of your experience. Somebody like the pathologist has to deal efficiently with dead people at his job, but when he goes home he's got to leave his work at work.

So it was important to alter his amnesia and what he remembered. He chunked too big. He chunked pictures— "If I don't see any pictures I don't have any problems." That was too big a chunk. So people in his group were asking him to make pictures but he wouldn't do it. You could hardly blame him. So they gave him a more refined way to sort in his mind.

One of the challenges I give students is to figure out how to fix a phobia in someone who is afraid of making images of himself. That's how I can tell who's good at NLP and who's weak. Because if people can only do it with the old phobia cure, they're stuck.

Don't ever expect that either they have to pretend
or that they realize that they are making images
. . . they are the exaggerated case. Those are the
ones who are the best to work with. They are the
ones who are making an image respond to its
input. And if you can have them look at white or
black, and find out which way it goes . . . if it's
getting brighter or dimmer. Some people dim
down and get so intense that they don't want to
look at them. Those are the people with white
backgrounds. So what else did you do? He got his
phobia. What did you guys do? Get bored now
with old shit. I'm not interested in that. Did you
change it and get him where you wanted? You
can just change it without working on it. Alter or
change it, I don't want this working on it. It's like
working through it. You can't stop from working
through these problems. You can't stop from
thinking that you have to work through these terrible problems. You enjoy it, that's true, but I
work through . . . I just don't like the way it
sounds. You can change the way you talk or I'll
torture you.

Group	I'll back down.
Richard	We haven't answered free-floating phobia now. Have you ever had a phobia?
Group	No.
Richard	Well, we can't just leave them lying around. We have to give them to people who deserve them.

I have enough problems. I'm not going to California. I'm going back to Hawaii.

Group   You actually pick somebody when you want to take revenge?

Richard   Shit, why not? Hey, you know, people . . . I do it all the time. And we can do it covertly and be good at it. The question is, do you value your stage in life? Or do you want to be rash with such an area of your life? Careful my friend. In order to clear up things at this point, I want you first of all to realize that the last four days were to get here. You have a toy you can go and play with in lots of different ways. But what I'm interested in is not how you're going on the road . . . What I want to find out is change . . . contrast, color. Look at your TV set. I'll tell you, you want to trip out some of your friends? Somebody comes over and you're watching TV, you walk up to the dials on there and act like you can't get the reception right. Change the contrast and brightness while something's going on. Just sort of while you're talking to them and watch. You can figure out all these things, like if it gets brighter, do they get more involved? If it gets dimmer, do they not get as involved? You can start doing things with people who *REALLY* respond quickly to any change in brightness. How many of you have rheostats in your house? How many of you only have them in the bedroom? Things that control lights that can get brighter or dimer. There are the people that have three-way bulbs. They don't respond as intensely. Yes, well, think about the person that

you live with. Maybe your rheostat will go a long
way. There are things like that . . . people have
sets in their dining rooms a lot. If you get two
people where one goes brighter as it gets more
intense and the other . . . when it goes dimmer it
gets more intense, this is where you want to find
the perfect balance. And, of course, that's the time
where you get one to close their eyes and you
turn the lights way up. *Ahhhhhh* . . . there is com-
promise in life. The thing is . . . is that you also
can make certain areas where you respond differently to the context of what's going on. If you
have disagreements with partners in your life,
there's a way of changing them. Here's a way of
changing yourself, instead of them. You can make
yourself like things you didn't like before. There's
an incredible wealth of things that you can do
with this. The hardest part is knowing where to
begin. So the thing that makes it something that
you can really get a handle on is that it's an
adventure . . . you can find out. You've acquired
a set of tools that are sophisticated and simple. Of
course you don't have . . . to do this with everybody all day long. That would be too boring. You
can vary the hell out of this. Why not try to make
a client worse, just for once? Make him worse for
a week. What the hell? They can do it, why not
you? Next week, then you can be a miracle person. This week will be worse. Really, you are a
master of what you can do. When you can induce
a phobia or take one away, then you are a master
of technology. You don't have to leave it there
unless it's for a good reason. Those of you who

are mothers who have teenage daughters with boyfriends, you now have a choice. Because people are, as far as I'm concerned, just like children: in a constant state of learning. As they get older there's more in there to work with, not less. It's harder to change a system that's in there unless you work with the system itself. Children are just *arrrrrh,* you can teach them anything, but half the time you don't know what you're teaching. With adults you can be a little bit more methodical, a little bit more direct. Use that relevancy thing, about if you're going to quit smoking because you want to feel better *na, na, na, na,* stuff like that. Don't have somebody tap dancing with red shoes on as the image of what that would be like if they were in that state. Just like I did with the lady who was sitting back there. She's sitting over there now. Use it for an anchor for them. She didn't like being controlled by this desire. When she was in control of the desire, there's certain things she would get out of it. She doesn't like being controlled by the worms. She can even let bugs crawl over her and it doesn't bother her.

Group   That's never happened, never . . .

Richard   It can be done. The most important thing is being able to laugh about it when it occurs. 'Cause anything that seems serious to you, if you can sit down and laugh at it and play with it, you can alter it and change it. That technology is becoming available to you. If they know how to fix a car, sure. You can get them to want to learn how to fix your car. Especially those of you who are clinicians. To teach them how to take care of themselves. So when they have problems in the future they can do it. This lady back here, I forgot your name again, Eileen. What happens is you don't wear name tags. She knows her name. Well, if I didn't know your name then something terrible happens. In the night. In the dark. Suddenly a tall image appears in the air. Flutters down and goes *CHOCOLATE, CHOCOLATE, ohhhhhhh-hhhhh.* She doesn't only have something that compulsively bears her in the other direction. But the thing she's really got that's valuable is that when she finds something else in her life where she's out of control, she's got the technology to do something about it without me. And to me, that's when what you do counts. Not when you stop somebody from smoing. It's when you teach them how to use their mind. You will have to figure out how to make money off of it. Or you're going to have to be paid to be someone's friend. Because you're going to have the technique, so you don't need to . . . unless you have something else left to teach them, which I think you will by then. You'll be able to make up all kinds of wild and crazy things. They won't be coming to be repaired. They'll be coming to be ultimized. We just made a whole new concept. You can get out of the business of repairing and get into the business of modification or, by my auto mechanic. He says, "I do not run a repair shop. . . I do not repair cars, I optimize them. If you want your car repaired give it to someone else." Whereas he makes the car the best it can be.

My car is two years old. It's a lot better than the day I bought it. I bet that they're not too many of you who can say that about your automobile. That mechanic has what I consider to be the attitude of the neuro-linguistic programmer. You go out and have a good time. The next time Robert comes back, don't you let him get serious on you or he'll drown you with words. You guys party if he gives you a hard time. I'm even considering sending a weirdo with him that I know. Dressed up a little bit. Robert, of all the people I know, is the one who knows more about this technology than anybody else. I could sit down and explain this to him in the most esoteric terms in the world, and he turns around and fixes a schizophrenic. Explaining a schizophrenic and selling a car to Robert are not different. He is in a sense the true neuro-linguistic programmer. He will of course expect you to be there too. He paces the same way I do. Pace me. But that's what pacing really is. Pacing is where I can make it so that it's possible for you to go at my rate, because after a while if I went at each of your individual rates, I'd have to talk to the class thirty different times. So go out and have so much fun and come back with wild and crazy stories. Find out how many phobias you can fix. I want each of you to do at least five phobias, even if they're unwilling strangers. And I want each of you to take somebody who claims they want to quit smoking and get them to stop. When you come back in here, I want each of you to have done five at a minimum. And look at Robert and say, "Robert, you're supposed to ask if everybody in here has gotten somebody to quit smoking." Because I don't want to hear this shit about smoking any more. We've got that one . . . it's done. And I want you guys to go out and do a five-year follow-up study to prove that it will only take a month. Go out and get somebody to stop smoking who wants to quit smoking. Then we don't have to worry about smoking. We can get down to more exquisite things. Like making your personal sexual lives more exquisitely exciting than anybody has ever conceived in the world. Let's get down to the good stuff. And I'll see you guys in the future.

Chapter 5

Beyond Beliefs

The next two demonstrations offer examples from what I consider the most comprehensive study in NLP, the changing of beliefs.

The beliefs people have about themselves, their potential, about how good their lives can be, or how capable of passion and success they are will guide their lifestyles. The important thing to realize is that these beliefs are not based on reality or truth, but on how we use our own biology. These beliefs are made up of the feelings and pictures we make and the things we tell ourselves.

The following transcripts show how a good understanding of accessing cues, internal states and the size and location of pictures allows the NLP practitioner to change beliefs quickly and effectively.

I want the reader to consider what it would mean to be able to take beliefs—for instance, that anything is possible to achieve, or that tomorrow is going to be a happy day—and make them as solid as your belief that the sun is coming up in the morning.

Imagine believing that so pervasively that you went around putting a smile on people's faces rather than worrying about the trivia most of us are worrying about.

If you step up and take control of your cognitive processes; when you realize that you can turn phobias on and off, that you can make pictures bigger and smaller, that you can literally take something from your past, push it into the distance and make it seem like it was a long time ago, then you can begin to think of things that you couldn't even conceive of wanting or having before.

When you consider the possibilities, when you start peeking on the outside of the future rather than going back to clean up the past, then it's bonus time. That's when you get the E-ticket rides and your life becomes a full-tilt boogie.

————————

Richard   Another approach to change is to examine the
               things that you believe about yourself, which you
               wish you didn't. These beliefs also can serve you,
               because if you didn't believe this or that about
               yourself, you'd be able to do things, and engage in
               things, and enjoy things, that you can't now . . . .
               the question is, how do you know when you're
               having a belief? (Laughter). That's a good
               question. (Points to woman 1 who is nodding
               yes.) How do you know when you're having a
               belief? Since you think it's a good question. Well
               . . .

Woman   I think it is such a good question.

Richard	Do *YOU* have something that you believe about yourself, that you wish you didn't? (Laughter).
Woman	Something that I believe about myself?
Richard	*Yeah,* that you believe, I mean really strongly believe.
Woman	I can't say it right here.
Richard	This is just a yes-no question, not a request for a description that would lead us to show you for life.
Woman	Yes. I do.
Richard	Alright (Laughter.) (Rolls his eyes.) Don't, don't go off on anything long here. (Laughter.) BUT . . . (Laughter.) You have something, no matter what it is. You have something that you believe about yourself. Do you have a really strong belief? You don't want any of these dipshit beliefs. (Laughter.) (She nods yes.) Okay. Now. How do you know you believe it? How do you know you have the belief in the first place?
Woman	I believe I have evidence that it's true.
Richard	Okay, well, if you, when you think about the belief, do you have, perhaps (humorous tone) some internal image that comes to mind? (Taps his foot and hand as if saying, "Big deal. Let's get on with it.") (Woman nods yes.)
	You have a belief, right? Right? Now, is it a strong belief? Now what makes it so, that you can

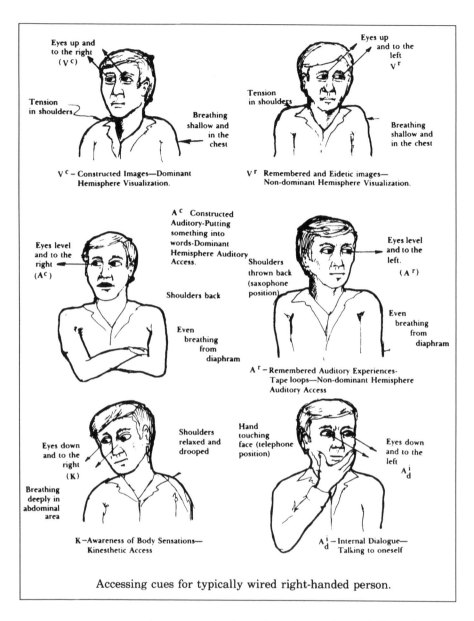

Accessing cues for typically wired right-handed person.

say it's strong, is that there's evidence? But, in the meanwhile, you know you have this belief, in fact you've got to have more than this one, and you've gotta have a way of knowing which beliefs are which. You don't, you know, forget you have this belief, do you? You have to remind yourself so you might perhaps make pictures or talk to yourself or have certain feelings. That kind of stuff. Okay? (She nods.) Alright? So I just have this intuition that there was a picture. I don't know . . . (Laughter.) There, there was something that I saw that made me feel that way. (Laughter.) Okay. Was there, in fact, a picture. Okay. Now. Stop and think about something that you kind of don't believe. I mean not, you know, it's, ah, just take something that you believe that could go one way or the other. I mean, it's like, you know, you believe that you want to have something for lunch but you can't get it for lunch. It's not a strong belief. Okay. (She nods.) Now pick something about yourself that you doubt is the case, that you wish was true. Now go inside and compare the strong belief with the thing that you have doubt about. Are they different? (She nods.) Surprise. Alright. For example, what are some of the differences?

Woman   How many things are in the picture? The darkness, the color, there's less color.

Richard   Are the pictures the same size?

Woman   Uh huh.

Richard   Alright. So both pictures are the same size?

Woman   No. Hmmm . . . Not proportionally. I mean they take up the same amount of space in my head but one's big and one's little. (Laughing, Richard makes a face as if she's not making sense.) I know what I'm talking about. (Group laughter.)

Richard   We'll see. (Laughter).

Woman   I don't know.

Richard   Now, when you say they're the same size, but proportionally aren't the same, are you telling me that one is, that in terms of the amount of space they take up, they're the same? That one is closer, farther away than the other, for example?

Woman   Yes.

Richard   Okay, see. It's not so hard. It's just when they take up the same amount of space, but they're not the same size. (Laughter). That means that you didn't know what you were talking about. (Laughter). The thing is, is that they are the same size but they're different distances. Okay.

            Did they appear to actually be more distant from one another? Or is it a more distant shot?

Woman   More distant shot.

Richard   Okay. Now. Which one is which? The strong belief is closer. (She nods.) Okay. And this is something you believe about yourself to be true. Do you want to believe that it's true? (She shakes head no.) Okay. Guess what you do. (Richard rolls up his sleeves.) (Laughter). Oh Santa . . . (Mimics tone of small child). (Laughter). Alright, we'll try it. (She smiles). Push the picture back. Is that enough? There's got to be a little bit more distance from this belief. Now. Push, as you push it back do you have growing doubts? (She laughs teasingly.) Really makes you believe in reality doesn't it? (Laughter). Well that takes care of that. Another sixty seconds of therapy. If you know what you're doing, therapy doesn't take that long. But see, then there's the thing about making it last. So stop and think about it now. Do you still believe that it's true? (She nods yes.) Alright now. The trick is, is being able to know how to push it back and make it stay that way. For example, if I wanted to be tricky right now, for example, is there something you would like in its place? Do you know what you'd like to believe? (She smiles and nods yes.) Okay. Now when you look at that, does that look different? 'Cause you obviously don't believe that. Okay. Is it perhaps, more off in the distance? (Laughter). Okay. (She nods yes.) Well? Is it, is it brighter perhaps? (She nods yes.) Okay, well now. Let me ask you what you think would happen if you were to push back the one that you don't want to believe and right out of the center of it would come up the other one you want to believe? And as you pushed one back that you didn't want, it became brighter, and the one that came through the center and just opened up like that, (gestures with hands) became darker. What do you think would happen? Now.

Woman   I guess, I . . .

Richard   I know.

Woman	That would, that. The one in the back was supposed to become brighter or the one coming out of the middle was supposed to become brighter, right?
Richard	Well the one coming out of the middle is the one you want, right?
Woman	Right.
Richard	Okay. It should become a little darker because you told me that things you believed were darker. That's what you told me.
Woman	Oh, okay, yeah.
Richard	Alright. Just follow the instructions. (Laughter). Just do it real fast. Just like that. (Moves right hand forward-left hand back.) Real quick. Now. So that it's going to stay that way, *hasn't* it? (Laughter).
Woman	So far.
Chris	Thank you. (Laughter).
Richard	That's right. Well they always say thank you too soon. That's called running away.
Chris	I know. Have to make sure.
Richard	Okay. Now stop and think about it. (Pause). Okay. Now stop and think about the thing that you believed was true before. *Didn't you?* It was a very strong belief, *wasn't it?* (Laughter).

Chris   That's great.

Richard   Huh, well, it's it's, it's very easy now. But to be
               able to know how to do that and with just which
               things [submodalities] to do it and with whom, is
               not always as simple as it appears until you know
               how. Once you know how then things are always
               easy. So I want to ask you to just be a little careful
               that you don't jump to use this too quickly. And
               also that you're careful about which beliefs you do
               it with. Um, you know, 'cause there's some
               beliefs that are best left alone (turns to her) and
               best changed. (She smiles, beaming.)

Richard   (Throws her a kiss and winks.)

───────────

Richard   . . . Once I put for my profession on my credit
               application, 'killer of sacred cows.' (Laughter).
               Okay, when you're having a belief, how do you
               know you have one? Do you know you have
               them?

Man   If you don't know . . . that you have at least one
               belief, then you've got one.

Richard   It's a clever answer, but it's not good enough—
               not here. (Laughter).

Man   That's right.

Richard   Well, do you know of a belief you have?

Man   I believe Richard Bandler's pretty competent in
            his business.

Richard   Okay. How do you know you have that belief?

Man   I've observed him working with people.

Richard   No, we're not talking about him. We're talking
            about your belief.

Man   Oh, and right now I have the belief. I keep
            spending my money to come back. (Laughter).

Richard   That's how I *know* he has the belief! (Laughter).

Man   And also, the people, I go back and tell them.
            'Yeah, I was there . . . was working with Richard
            Bandler,' they believe too. (Laughter). We all
            have a lot of belief.

Richard   You have to be careful. You can be lynched for
            that kind of talk. (Laughter).

Man   I . . . I live in a very isolated area. Maui's very
            isolated.

Richard   Oh, in Maui, that's different. (Laughter). Yeah, I
            don't go to Maui, so I don't have that problem.
            People in Kona still haven't figured out what I do
            for a living. They always ask, "What do you do
            for a living?' And I say, "Well, ah . . . you know,
            Neuro-linguistic programming.' And they go,
            'Yeah, what's that?' And I said, 'It's kind of like
            surfing, but safer. (Laughter). You know, it's
            where you change your mind.' And they go, 'Ah,

I've done that.' (Laughter). Naw, actually I decided to make life over there very easy. I told them I was a retired plumber. And there was an excess of plumbers, so I don't have people asking me things like that. (Laughter). Actually, I . . . they, people asked if I was an M.D., and I said, 'Yes, a manic depressive. Licensed by the state of California. Depressed here, manic over there.' (Laughter). Well, how do you know if . . . that you have that belief?

Man	Ah, two or three things caught them. One is the (Richard-Ah, yes) One of the things is . . . (Richard-What's up there?)
Richard	Well, alright, you stopped and your eyes shifted up. I have an intuition that you made a picture. (Laughter). No. You didn't see anything when you looked up there?
Man	It depends on (eyes go up again) . . . yes.
Richard	It's okay. It's your subjectivity, not mine.
Man	In my subjectivity, I have a conviction.
Richard	Okay, how do you know when you have one? What's a *conviction* made out of?
Man	For me over kinesthetic representation. (feelings in NLP jargon).
Richard	Okay, so you have a feeling. Alright. How do you know what the feeling is about?

Man   Ah, it allows me to organize the world.

Richard   Okay, but when you have the feeling, how do
               you know what subject the feeling is about? Since
               you have more than one conviction. How do you
               know when you're convinced about one thing as
               opposed to another?

Man   . . . the other belief about . . .

Richard   Okay but . . . alright, you have a feeling, okay.
               How does the feeling tell you what the subject is?
               Do you talk to yourself in words, or make
               pictures, or I mean . . . what internal representa-
               tion do you have that allows you to know that
               you have a conviction about this as opposed to
               that?

Man   Well, I guess I make pictures.

Richard   Okay, now. If you stop and think about one thing
               that you have a conviction about, okay, what's
               the structure of what it is that you detect
               internally? What about the rest of you? Give you
               a minute to think about that. See, this is really the
               subject to me right now, for the evening. Was
               . . . if you're going to deal with beliefs, the ques-
               tion is . . . for example, some of you have beliefs
               which are very strong, as opposed to ones which
               could go either way. I mean, you may have a
               belief about what it is that you want to eat for
               dinner. Or a belief about what you want to do
               during the course of an evening. And that belief
               can be changed very easily. Whereas there are

other beliefs which are very very strong, and last for a long time. Now, how do you know when you are having a belief? You guys want me to come back tomorrow, or . . . (shrugs shoulders) (laughter). Well, stop and think about a belief that you have. When you stop and think about the beliefs . . . alright. If you think about a belief you have, what do you do inside your head when you're thinking about it? (Points to someone else.) You pick a very strong belief that you have. How do you know you have that belief?

Woman   I feel it.

Richard   Okay. Well, you have a feeling. Now (slowly) how do you know which belief it is? (rapidly) You have more than one strong belief.

Woman   It's strong.

Richard   Okay, alright . . . (One word at a time) now how do you know what the subject of the belief is?

Woman   Because that's the strongest feeling I have.

Richard   Well, how do you know which . . . *which feeling it is?*

Woman   I . . . hear?

Richard   You hear something. You tell yourself, like, what? Like what do you tell yourself, for example?

Woman   I tell myself the belief's there and that it's real.

Richard   Okay, now. How do you know what to tell your-
            self? If I ask you to think of a strong belief, do you
            go inside and go, 'A strong belief?' And then a
            voice answers you and names something?

Woman   No. I listen to myself . . . describe what my basic
            core is.

Richard   Okay. Now, do you have more beliefs than just
            that one?

Woman   Yeah, but that's a simple one.

Richard   Okay, now, when you think about another belief
            you have, do you do the same thing?

Woman   Yeah. (Nonchalantly).

Richard   Okay. How do you know what to say? Okay,
            when you're saying what the core belief is.

Woman   Yeah. (Richard-Right.) I hear myself saying it.

Richard   Okay. How do you know what to say?

Woman   Ah . . . from a host of chemical anonymous past
            human experience.[1]

Richard   Okay, do you go through those somehow?

---

1. "From a host of chemical anonymous past human experience." I had already told
these people that their experiences were basically chemical, and that chemical shifts in
the brain enable people to reaccess memories.
    "Anonymous" means she's not taking control over these memories. It's like
they're somebody else's memories.

Woman	Very quickly.
Richard	Okay, well that's sort of what we do here in these seminars . . . is deal with these things. You know, so you very quickly go through. Do you do that auditorily also, or do you happen to do that visually?
Woman	No, I have the feeling.
Richard	Okay, well you have the feeling. And you just run through a bunch of feelings?
Woman	Yes.
Richard	Okay . . . and there aren't any pictures attached to them?
Woman	One. (Richard mimics eye movements.) (Blushes). (Laughter).
Richard	(Smiling). One. (Laughter). For each feeling? Is it a slide or a movie?
Woman	No, this is just one at a time. Hangs in this little wall. For this particular belief.
Richard	Okay, alright. So you have one. Is it a slide or a movie?
Woman	It's just there. It's a slide.
Richard	It's just a still picture?
Woman	Yes. But it's dimensional.

Richard   Okay. Holographic. Now. When you have . . .
             when you stop and think of a belief you have
             that's now **that** strong . . .

Woman   Oh, okay.

Richard   Alright, now. How do you know you have that
             belief?

Woman   Um. It's not that I have much of a question, and
             then I go, 'Yeah, well whatever' and then that
             feels bad so then I go look until it feels good.

Richard   (Exaggerated patience). Okay, but how do you
             know what the subject of it is?

Woman   Because of what I . . . because then I feel, like if I
             told, I started feeling. That's all I need. And then I
             say to myself . . .

Richard   (Mimics that this makes sense nodding yet
             portraying with humor this sounds nuts to get her
             on track) How do you know what the need is
             when you feel it?

Woman   Well, and like this if I can't decide (makes face) I
             go, 'Hmm, you know,' and I know . . .

Richard   You say one, and then say the other, and then one
             has the stronger feeling attached to it?

Woman   I feel a whole bunch. I feel a whole bunch. I
             whine, I . . . (gestures could be or not) And then
             all of a sudden something . . . and I go . . .

Richard   Okay, whereas that's very . . .

Woman   (Eyes up). And one comes up.

Richard   Now . . . but with a strong belief, when you say
               it (snap) you have a very solid feeling?

Woman   Centered. (Word implies overdose of therapy and
               means yes.)

Richard   Centered feeling. Okay. Now, when you have
               the feeling, are you looking at that picture?

Woman   No.

Richard   Okay. So. You just have a solid feeling?

Woman   Sometimes I can look up and see the picture too.

Richard   Well that's so, at least you know what . . . what
               the solid feeling is about.

Woman   Yeah.

Richard   Otherwise somebody could tell you, you know,
               that it was about buying a car from them. You
               know.

Woman   Got one that doesn't quite match.

Richard   Yeah, what doesn't it match?

Woman   My picture.

Richard   It doesn't match your picture. Okay now. As you
               change . . . can you look at that picture? Okay.

Now that particular slide picture . . . how is that different from other pictures that you have? If you make a picture of something else . . . alright. You made the slide of, let's say, beer as opposed to wine. If you make a slide of beer, do you have a solid feeling?

Woman   No. Little bitty picture.

Richard   Little bitty pictures. And the other one is a bigger picture? What happens if you make the picture of the beer just as big?

Woman   I don't want to. (Laughs). Um . . .

Richard   Does it change the way you feel?

Woman   Yeah. But we don't want to replace what I've got up there with beer.

Richard   Okay. But, but . . .

Woman   I don't want to.

Richard   You don't want to. The question is, can you?

Woman   I probably could.

Richard   Okay now. Do you have big pictures up there of beliefs that you have that you wish you didn't have? In other words, wasn't one of the things you did today, to think of things that you believed about yourself that you wish weren't the case? Can you think of one of those?

Woman	From what I just heard you say, as soon as you said that I saw something else completely then I thought of today. What happened today . . .
Richard	Okay now. Can you go up and look at that one and shrink it?
Woman	The big one?
Richard	Yeah, the one that you don't like.
Woman	Yeah.
Richard	What happens as you shrink it? Does it reduce the intensity of your belief?
Woman	Yes. (Startled).
Richard	(Sarcastic, but with pointed humor). Does it, so to speak, become a smaller idea?
Woman	Yeah.
Richard	What happens if you shrink it all the way down to where the picture is just a dot?
Woman	Then that changes . . . my whole thing is okay.
Richard	(As if a sudden emergency occurs) Well, hold on here. (Laughter). I can tell we're going to get into this one. (Laughter). It's like your thing that's it okay which is dots.
Woman	Yeah. (Laughter).

Richard	I'm sorry, can you go explain this a little further to me? Something is okay when it's just a dot?
Woman	As long as I'm looking at it.
Richard	Okay. (Nodding as if this makes sense but making faces.) (Laughter) . . . . If you have to look at it. Alright, now, if you stop and think about that belief that you shrunk into a dot, do you still believe that's true about you?
Woman	Um. Ah, yeah it's . . . it's there a little bit, but yeah, I can handle it now.
Richard	Okay, that takes care of that. (Laughter). Now you know what it is that I'm doing here.
Man	Finding things in each submodality. Sure we can't go with this thing . . . (Laughter).
Richard	You get the point of this. (Laughter). Now the purpose of what we do here is to get you to be able to drive your own bus. When you say just changing the submodality, is that what I did? Just change the submodality?
Man 1	No, no. You identified it.
Man 2	You changed the submodality so it went away . . . other things changed as it comes.
Richard	When you take a picture and turn it into a dot, are you just changing a submodality?
Woman	Yes and no.

Richard	Something like that, yeah. See the question is, what makes a belief last? In other words, you have to be able to make the distinctions so you don't forget what you believe from day to day. Although there are those who do that, too. (Laughter). Now, if you want a belief to be a big strong belief that lasts, you need to know, with each individual, especially with yourself, what it is that does that. See, for example, are there things that you would like to believe about yourself that you don't?
Woman	Yeah.
Richard	Think of one. And what . . . what does it look like? Is it a big picture? Isn't it? (Laughter). It was a small picture, wasn't it?
Woman	Yeah.
Richard	Do you believe it?
Woman	It depends on (mumbles).
Richard	Well, what are you waiting for? So the ones that you believe your . . . you see yourself in them?[2]
Woman	Like what?
Richard	(Imitating street jive from ghetto) Say what, here.
Woman	(Mimics) Say what?

---

2. (mumbles) . . . "Well, what are you waiting for? So the ones you believe your . . . you see yourself in them?" In other words, she believes those images in which she sees herself, which is why she is so confused in the first place. She doesn't believe direct experience, only distorted experience.

Richard	Okay, you remember you had a belief that *you* believed. And you still do. That's one that . . .
Woman	The little one?
Richard	Not the little one, the one that's the core belief.
Woman	Oh yeah.
Richard	Do you see yourself in that?
Woman	Ah, part of it.
Richard	You see yourself in part of that picture? You told me it was one still.
Woman	Oh no, I've never been in part of that. I know I am. (Laughter).
Richard	Well it's your core belief, not mine. (Laughter).
Woman	I know when we looked at it before . . .
Richard	Well, we'll wait here. Do you see yourself in the picture or not? Would you get me a glass of water, Chris?
Woman	Um. I can feel a whole . . . you know that.
Richard	I know.[3] You keep telling us that. But the question is, how do you get the feeling so well? Aren't

3. I can see what her answer is going to be, so I'm just jumping ahead. It really helps with people who are not very verbal if you're good at submodality elicitation. I know what her answer is going to be before she does.

there other things that you would like to feel that strongly about? (Laughter).

Woman   Um.

Richard   (Humorous sarcasm) Ah, probably not. (Laughter). There are other things that you'd like to feel that strongly about. Isn't it . . . there. Now.

Woman   Um huh.

Richard   Okay, now the question is, do you see yourself in *that* slide or not?

Woman   Hmmmm.

Richard   Well, you have to look at the picture. You're either there or you're not there.

Woman   Oh, I am there. I'm in. (Laughter).

Richard   Alright. Now go back and think of a thing that you would like to believe about yourself strongly.

Woman   Okay.

Richard   Do you see yourself in that one?

Woman   Yes. And when I got to that big one, I got in the little one.

Richard   Is it still smaller?

Woman   The small and the big one?

Richard   Yeah.

Woman   Um.

Richard   Was it that small?

Woman   No. It was smaller than the big one. The big one was my main one.

Richard   It *was*. Okay. As you look at them now, are they both the same size?

Woman   If I can bring it over. Sure (points right). If I bring them over that way then it's okay.

Richard   Yeah. Is it? Look . . . look at one and then look at the other. Are they both as big?

Woman   Yeah.

Richard   (To Chris) Thank you. Okay, do you believe both as strongly?

Woman   Doing what?

Richard   Do you believe both of them as strongly?

Woman   Um . . . not that both of them are the same . . . the feelings of belief as strongly as the belief is strong.

Richard   Yeah?

Woman   Yeah.

Richard   Okay. Well that wasn't hard, was it?

Woman   Um huh.

Richard   Okay, you wanted to believe it about you. Do
            you believe it now?

Woman   Yeah.

Richard   Okay. (Laughter).

Woman   Thank you very much. (Laughter). That's neat.
            You're okay, you know, for just being Richard
            Bandler and all that stuff. (Laughter). [Background
            talking and laughing].

Richard   Of course, there is the question about which
            beliefs are worth having. (Laughter).

Woman   I like mine.

Richard   Good. Now. What's important is to be able to do
            that with someone so that it works and it lasts. It's
            not just changing submodalities, it's finding out
            what makes it a strong belief. Which particular
            element . . . testing those elements, by seeing if
            you can reduce a belief and strengthen a belief by
            finding out specifically which are the elements in
            the submodalities that make it last, and then hav-
            ing them change quickly. Kind of like the swish
            pattern.

Woman   But you know what?

Richard   What?

Woman   It was the area that I . . .

Richard   Yes you were. Well yes, that's what makes it
               work. Yeah. That's sort of what I was telling
               them. (Laughter). You . . . you said it very
               succinctly. And you demonstrated very succinctly
               that you, in fact, didn't want to look at it. You
               kept saying, 'But I can feel it stronger.' 'Is there a
               picture?' And you went, 'No.' (Laughter). See,
               we're supposed to notice those things. Like, you
               know, eye accessing movements. You guys ever
               heard of that?

Man   Ahhhh.

Richard   Ummmm. Let me think about that, yeah. Or not.

Woman   Or not. (Laughter).

Richard   See, the point is . . . is if it is what builds a belief
               to have a lot of strength. Their natural inclination
               is to not mess with it. Makes it too easy to be able
               to have things be the way you would like them to
               be. (Laughter). Now, how do you go about find-
               ing one of these? Same way you go about finding
               everything else. By comparing it, yeah, by asking
               them to compare it with something which is not
               that strong a belief. You want to begin to find out
               what are the elements that make it different, not
               the things that are the same, but the things which
               are different between the strongest kind of belief
               they can have and the ones that really don't make
               a difference. Because if they have a belief that
               does make a difference about something, it's
               going to be partially like the other. 'Cause there
               are beliefs which are not as strong as the core

belief, and not as much as a belief about what you would like to have for dinner. But those will be harder for you to make the distinctions with about what really counts. The more diverse the case is, in other words, the more it could, eh . . . could go either way: I could have this for dinner or that for dinner. That will be much different from what the core beliefs are. So it will give you a much greater indication of exactly what needs to be changed. Now. Do you understand what I did? Good. 'Cause you're going to do it. That's why they call them work . . . shops. (Laughter). How are you doing, Coleman? Well there's, yeah . . . do you have a question?

Man   Yeah, the question is, ah . . . my question, when you approach one of those deeply held beliefs . . .

Richard   That what?

Man   When you approach, when one . . . when I approach one of the deeply held beliefs . . . (Richard-Yeah.) people begin to say things like, or feel things like, 'If you took that away from me I would not exist.'

Richard   They're right.

(Man-So?)

Don't take it away from them. Because they're right. The point is not to take away, the point is to add. The point is not to take her core belief and shrink it down. The thing is . . . is to take a belief that she doesn't want to have about herself, first, and shrink it down. And then go from shrinking it down to replacing it with what she would like to believe. Otherwise you don't leave people anything.

Woman   How do you know . . .

Richard   Well, you don't have to. It's always nice though. See, the thing is . . . is if somebody has a belief about himself that he doesn't like. The fact that he doesn't like it makes it not ecological for him to start with. Now if you want to be sure that you check the ecology of the change, then what you need to do is to find out, as you begin to take that belief and shrink it, if it has difficulty. For example, if it was, in her case, it's shrinking it. In other people's cases it'll be something different. As you begin to ask them to alter it, if they begin to become unnerved it's a very good indication that what you're doing is taking away from something without having already prepared something to put there. See, before I did that with her I stopped and said, 'Think of something that you would like to believe about yourself.' Now, as you take one away and replace it with something else, if you have difficulty doing it, it's because the rest of them object. And at that point in time, hopefully you have a variety of choices. One would be to find out what it is that they're talking about. For example, if their belief is that they can fly . . . yeah, well we . . . they can jump off the bridge over here. Now there are people in this world, you know, who, under certain drugs or in the waking state will say, you know, 'I can fly, I can fly,' who are wrong. Now, that means that it is possible to make an unecological change. In this case the people in here, I think, should be able to notice that and to have some back-up resources. For example, have you ever heard of, oh what's it called, umm . . . re something or other? (Laughter).

Man Reblaming?

Richard Yes. Reblaming, that's what it was. (Laughter). That's where if it's not ecological you blame someone else in your family. (Laughter). Okay. The ecological check is going to come by waiting after you do it for a period of five minutes or so, and then having them go back and find out if it's still there. For example, think about it now. Okay, well, you wanted to believe something about yourself, right? Do you still believe it?

Woman Oh, yes. But I wanted to tell you it's like how . . . it came like you . . .

Richard In English please. (Laughter).

Woman When I put the big, little picture up here. The thing I didn't want to actually look at, 'cause I wasn't very visual before that, I believe. And put a little dot right here in the center. (Richard-Yeah) And then you said, 'Well what's the thing you believe the most of? The thing right here?' (Richard-Yeah) Okay. But little thing . . . I put the little thing, the visual thing, right there. That little spot . . . (Richard-Yeah) Well, the big thing that was over here that I (Richard-Yeah) wanted to be . . . (Richard-Uh huh) that somehow I could feel, I put over here. But I had to . . . then when I moved them over here . . . (Richard-Yeah) okay, I move it and bring it into here. Bring it to me.

Richard   Bring it to you?

Woman   I feel it.

Richard   Yes?

Woman   Yes.

Richard   Okay.

Woman   But that little tiny thing that I didn't like before, it was so big all those years. That was also this humongous huge thing that I believe now, along with what I want to be in the future was . . . I can bring it all, all here now. That's where I am now.

Richard   That's clear. (Laughter.) But it is to me. It's called the swish pattern.

Man   Ah.

Richard   You know what that is, don't you?

Man   It's where you take a (Laughter) . . .[4]

Woman   So what did you say it was? (Laughter).

Richard   It was a swish pattern Do you know the swish pattern?

Woman	No.
Man	Yeah you do.
Woman	What . . . oh this thing?
Richard	Yeah. (Laughter).
Woman	No, I didn't know that. (Laughter).
Man	Right, right.
Richard	You know, where there's a square and you put one in the little corner and you make it bigger? You know that one.
Woman	Oh yeah.
Richard	Okay, well it's the same pattern that you used. You just didn't use squares.
Woman	A circle?
Richard	Yeah. That's . . . that's right. Um huh. How many times did you do it?
Woman	One, one, one good time.

---

4. "It's where you . . . " The group laughs because I'm making faces at them. When he says, "It's where you take . . . ", his accessing cues show that he looks at the picture; I just wipe it out with my hand. And when the other participant asked, "So what did you say it was?" I did the same thing. I say, "It was the swish pattern" take my hand and go *kshshsh* with their pictures, and they're done at that point. I literally fixed the picture so much that I could do the swish pattern with my hands with each of them. After that their questions are gone, because it changed their beliefs that fast.

A good knowledge of where people localize images in space gives you this kind of control over their internal experience.

Richard	One good time. How many times did you do it?
Woman	Say what?
Richard	Say what? Well you did it a couple of times before you got the one good one though, didn't you?
Woman	The . . . I don't know. How do you know? I did it once for sure.
Richard	'Cause I kept asking you to do it over and over again.
Woman	Did you?
Richard	Uh huh.
Woman	Oh. (Laughter) Well I . . .
Richard	And then I asked you to explain what it is that you did do . . . Okay, well, there's another one. (Laughter). Want to try for another? (Laughter). What was it that you didn't do more than once? (Laughter).
Woman	Every time I do it I feel it more. (Laughter). You wouldn't . . .
Richard	Yes. (Laughter). You know, somebody told me you couldn't do this covertly. (Laughter).
Woman	But how with each time I do it I . . .

Richard	We called it bootlegging where I came from. (Laughter). Okay. Do you understand what the task is now? [Background talking].
Woman	I have a question.
Richard	Yes ma'am.
Woman	Ah, what is the point in helping somebody to believe something about themselves which is about to . . . for example, I'm fat, I'm not a good, ah, tennis player, for example . . .
Richard	As opposed to . . . you would like to believe what?
Woman	For example, I would like to believe that I am a good tennis player. What good will it give to me if I believe that and it's not true?
Richard	Ah very little good at all.
Woman	Yes.
Richard	It would be much more useful to believe that you could *become* a good tennis player.
Woman	Oh. (Laughter).
Richard	If you didn't believe you could become a good tennis player, it's highly unlikely that you would even stand a chance.
Woman	Okay, so . . .

Richard   See most people do not . . . I agree with you.
               Most people do not come in and ask for things
               which are useful. They come in . . . people come
               in and they want to be confident. They very
               rarely come in and ask to become competent.
               And, ah . . . sort of the best way to go about that
               is to find out what it is that you're doing. In other
               words, what the belief is. And if you don't like it,
               ask . . . tell them to do something else. I mean, to
               me it's a lot more useful to get people to believe
               that they can learn to do something than to affirm
               the delusion that they already know how to. And
               I agree with that. And you can . . . you can usu-
               ally peg those people anyway, because they have a
               lot of beliefs which are sort of like that anyway.
               Ah, they show up in seminars a lot. They are the
               people who always talk about how, ah . . . I'll do
               something with submodalities and they'll go,
               'Well yeah, I already know submodalities.' You
               know. They've heard it once before so therefore
               they know how to do it. But the intricacies and
               the delicacies of being able to find out which ele-
               ments to work with specifically to get lasting
               results, that's where the real artistry comes from.
               The most sophisticated part of what I'm asking
               you to do is to find out precisely which element
               produces the change in belief that lasts. Knowing
               that, you can reduce a belief and replace it with
               one which is more functional. Just like that. My
               work is ninety five percent information gathering
               and five percent doing.

Man   It's the *kind* of information.

Richard	That's right. And being able to test all the information constantly as you get it. Constantly testing the quality of the information. If they tell you something about them, then have them try it and find out if it works. I mean, I tested it on a can of beer versus wine. And when she told me she didn't want to make this can of beer that big, that's the answer to your question. She said, 'I don't want the can of beer to be that big.' I said, 'Okay, let's pick something that you do.' But that's the indication, when people start telling you that they're going to lose their reality. That tells you you're right where you ought to be. It doesn't tell you to push through it. But it tells you that you're working with the right elements. And when you find things that they want there, and things that are useful, then they won't feel like they're going crazy. Then they feel like they're becoming better human beings. As opposed to crazy. And believe me, if anybody knows you can have the reality taken apart at the seams, this is the very room in which I used to do it with people. I used to run a seminar called the Fabric of Reality. We all got together and methodically dissected our ability to discern what was real and what was not real. That's why none of those people are here anymore. (Laughter).
Man	We are. (Laughter).
Richard	Huh? Well, we hopefully put them back together. In fact we put them back together in a slightly different way . . . in ways that build even stronger realities. 'Cause you need to have a good sense of

shared reality to be able to function. And part of what I'm asking you to do is to *extend* your shared reality so that the information you gather from another human being allows what you do to them to work, and for you to notice whether it works. Because you're sharing their reality, not forcing it one way or another, but being able to enter it and believe it. To test it and be able to affect it and change it. And that will allow you to do all kinds of things in this world. See, you can make yourself believe you're a great tennis player, but you're still gonna lose. But you can make yourself *believe* that you can be a great tennis player, and that it is enjoyable to practice. Then you will be a good tennis player and you will enjoy practicing. And that to me is a much more functional thing. Because even if you do lose you're going to enjoy the process. And that to me is more important than whether you can knock a ball over a net where somebody is not standing. (Laughter). Which is, ah . . . the American pastime is to get balls from here to there and over nets and back and forth. That's right, people here are obsessed with them. See, you know . . . oblong ones and round ones. They want to kick them here and there. And they want to stick balls in holes a lot. Somebody took me golfing. I'd never played golf. They didn't have golf courses where I came from. At least that they let us on. (Laughter). You know, they were afraid we'd steal the grass. (Laughter). And I went out to play golf, and they give you a little tiny stick and a little tiny ball, and then you have to hit it all the way down to try and get it in a hole. When you have a perfectly good golf cart to drive it down there and stick it in the hole! (Laughter). Seems quite silly to me. But it's one of the sports I like 'cause you can drink while you play golf (Laughter). That's why I always loved bowling, except for the part of picking up the heavy ball. (Laughter). You know, I always wanted to *shoot* the pins down. That seemed a lot easier to me. (Laughter). Okay. You have, ah . . . some people here to help you get through this if you get stuck, and ah . . . go for it.

Conclusion

I hope these examples will help students of NLP—for whom this book was primarily designed—to improve their skills, as well as help laymen understand how easily these changes can be made. People should realize that they have a right to expect, from any NLP practitioner or practitioner of any therapy, that change will be simple and straightforward.

Moshe Feldenkrais, one of the greatest communicators and healers of our time, told me once that the only things that work are the things that in the end seem so obvious that everyone should have known them all along. He called this the "elusive obvious," a term that I later chose, as his editor, for the title of his last book.

In years of working with people, I have found that whenever I had to struggle to produce change, it was because I was doing it the hard way. There really weren't many other ways, because the technology of change and mental cognition was still in its infancy.

NLP is a new science and art form that offers us tools to influence the specific processes by which we manipulate our subjective experience. The broad way to new choices is wide open.

Chapter 6

Weight Loss

Millie, the woman I work with in this demonstration, approached my secretary at lunch on the last day of a sales seminar.

She said that she had gained 20–25 pounds over the past few months and wanted to lose weight without becoming obsessed about dieting or making it into a life-consuming struggle. She wanted to either not worry about her weight or find something that would work.

Since I didn't have time to do it after the seminar, I suggested she come up on the stage as a demonstration subject at the end of the last day.

As in previous chapters, the weight isn't really the issue; the issue is to learn how to focus your attention.

The following transcripts contain three levels of patterning:

COLUMN 1: Transcript of client.

COLUMN 2: Linguistic patterns.

COLUMN 3: Sequences of experience and analog markers.

List of Abbreviations

CON	Conjunction	PHON. AMB.	Phonological Ambiguity
IC	Implied Causative	SYN. AMB.	Syntactic Ambiguity
CE	Cause-Effect	SCO. AMB.	Scope Ambiguity
MR	Mind Reading	EQ	Embedded Question
MRI	Missing Referential Index	EC	Embedded Command
SRV	Selectional Restriction Violation	QU	Quote
DEL	Deletion	PRE	Presupposition
UV	Unspecified Verb	CP	Conversational Postulate
NOM	Nominalization	FRA	Fragment

COLUMN 1

(1)

You! Come on down!

No need to be nervous!

(Ha, ha, ha, ha)

That's the establishing-rapport part.

(Laughter)

COLUMN 2

(1)

CP: No need to be nervous; DEL: nervous about what? MRI: That's...NOM: rapport, part; MRI: rapport, part

COLUMN 3

(1)

In addition to using commands I use the command tonality with each word; my tonality shifts down with each word.

The brain processes language by the phrase, not by the word. By using my intonation pattern to give each word the meaning of a sentence, I'm opening up the command module in the brain.

At the same time I pace her breathing, speak at the rate of my breathing, look her in the eye and go into a trance myself. She goes right with me. That's the easiest way to induce a trance.

(2)

Um. That's alright!

You don't need to breathe anymore,

I'll take care of that for you.

(2)

MRI: That's...DEL: alright for whom? what? CP: You don't need to breathe anymore; UV: take care...

(2-5)

Induction of a confusion state.

(3)

Okay, come in a little closer now, move a bit closer, within striking distance . . . and just sit back and relax.

(3)

PRE: little closer...bit closer...just; CON: and...EC: sit back...relax

(4)

We'll let the rest of you . . .

Um, for our general
purposes here there'll be
. . .

What I'm going to do is
. . .

Is not so important,

(4)

UV: let; FRA: We'll let the
rest of you . . . PRE: general . . . NOM: purposes
. . . PRE: here . . . UV:
will be . . . FRA: For our
general purposes here
there'll be . . . PRE: what
. . . UV: do . . . is . . .
FRA: what I'm going to do
is . . . PRE: not so much
. . . DEL: important to
whom?

(5)

and some of you will understand some of it, and some
of you won't.

(5)

MRI: some . . . PRE: some
. . . UV: understand . . .
MRI: some . . . it . . . some
. . .

(6)

Um, I mean basically . . .
basically what it boils down
to, in a nutshell, is that
everybody who . . . who's
ever tried to . . . to diet in
any way, realizes that it's
hard.

(6)

UV: mean . . . PRE: What
. . . is . . . basically . . .
MRI: it . . . UV: boils
down to . . . PRE: every-
body . . . UV: tried . . .
diet . . . PRE: realizes . . .
UV: realizes . . .

(6-7)

The contradiction in this
passage ("it's hard-it's easy")
intensifies the confusion
state.

(7)

And you know, it's people
that don't have any problem
dieting say it's easy, right
. . .

(7)

CON: And . . . MR: you
know . . . MRI: people . . .
PRE: any . . . NOM: prob-
lem . . .

(8)

I mean . . . like I have
friends that, you know, they
could go out, and eat everything in Orlando, right, and
they would never gain a
pound, and they always say
that dieting is easy.

(8)

UV: mean . . . MRI:
friends . . . MR: you know
. . . MRI: they . . . CON:
and . . . and . . . and

(8-16)

Suggestion of the possibility
of quickly learning to control your weight as soon as
you understand a few basic
principles.

(9)

I don't know why they do
it, though. This has always
surprised me.

(9)

UV: know . . . MRI: they
. . . This . . . PRE: always
. . . surprised; DEL: surprised how?

(10)

But there is something that
. . . that a friend of mine
figured out, a guy named
Don Wolfe.

(10)

CON: But . . . MRI:
something; PRE: figured
out . . .

(11)

He's a pretty good
hypnotist.

(11)

PRE: pretty good; DEL:
pretty good;

(12)

He . . . he was a student of
mine when I actually taught
at the university, and really
has concentrated on . . . on
dealing with one thing, and
that's being able to do
weight control in one day.

(12)

PRE: actually . . . really
. . . MRI: the university
. . . UV: concentrated . . .
MRI: one thing . . . that's
. . . UV:being able . . . do
. . . EC: do weight control
. . . NOM: weight, control;
PHON. AMB: weight -
wait;

(13)

Now, when he first told me
that I thought, "You got
weight off in one day? You
can only do that with an
axe," I said. "Just axe me
any question and I'll axe
you any answer."

(13)

PRE: first . . . UV: thought
. . . QU: "you got . . .
axe"; UV: got off . . . PRE:
only; UV: do . . . MRI:
that . . . QU: "Just . . .
answer." PRE: Just . . .
PHON. AMB.: Axe - ask;
MRI: any . . . any . . .
NOM: question, answer;

(14)

But the thing is that . . . is that, through all the research that's been done, doing things about controlling your metabolism to me are what I found to be the most important.

(14)

CON: But . . . MRI: the thing . . . PRE: the thing is that . . . all . . . NOM: research . . . MRI: research; UV: been done, doing; MRI: things? UV: controlling; NOM: metabolism; UV: found . . . DEL: most important compared to what?

(15)

And then understanding the four basic principles of what . . . of how to eat in order to lose weight:

(15)

CON: And . . . UV: understanding . . . PRE: basic . . . DEL: basic for what? NOM: principles . . . CE: eat in order to lose weight; EC: eat in order to lose weight; UV: lose . . . NOM: weight . . .

(16)

you eat only fresh foods, period. Nothing packaged, nothing canned, nothing dried, only food that is fresh, and you don't eat too much of it.

(16)

EC: eat only . . . PRE: only . . . fresh . . . nothing . . . nothing . . . nothing . . . only . . . CON: and . . . PRE: too much . . . MRI: it

(17)

Now, when my friend told me the basic principles of this, I roared with laughter because they are so simple—

(17)

IC: when my friend told me, I roared . . . MRI: the basic principles . . . this . . . NOM: principles, laughter; MRI: they . . .

(17-25)

Suggestion of the probability of successful weight control.

(18)

and you eat at the right times, and you know when those are, and other than that, you feel full, and exercise a little.

(18)

CON: and . . . and . . . and . . . EC: eat at the right times . . . MRI: right times; MR: you know . . . MRI: those . . . that . . . EC: feel full, exercise;

(19)

I mean, you don't have to go out and kill yourself, you know, walk a few blocks a day, you know, get up off your duff, and move around, you know,

(19)

UV: mean . . . MR: you know . . . EC: walk . . . get up . . . move around . . . DEL: walk, get up, move; MR: you know

(20)

go . . . take the stairs instead of the elevator a couple of times a day,

(20)

EC: go . . . take . . . MRI: the stairs, the elevator

(21)

and the other thing is . . . is to be able to change your metabolism.

(21)

CON: and . . . MRI: the other thing . . . PRE: other . . . UV: be able, change; NOM: metabolism; EC: change

(22)

Now, he and I just recently got together, and rented a studio.

(22)

PRE: just recently . . .

(23)

And we've made a tape, that, that's based on the fact that he does a group once a month, and bats .800 with weight control.

(23)

CON: And . . . UV: made . . . based . . . NOM: fact . . . UV: does . . . NOM: weight control

(24)

And he only sees people once and he sees them in a group.

(24)

CON: And . . . PRE: only . . . UV: sees . . . MRI: them . . .

(25)

Now that's a pretty good batting average.

(25)

MRI: that . . . DEL: pretty good compared to what?

(26)

And this is what he installs in people:

(26)

CON: And . . . MRI: this . . . PRE: this is what . . . SRV: installs in people

(26-35)

Induction of a curiosity state and introduction of the notion of automatic, unconscious processes that control behavior.

(27)

Now the only difference is, is there's a difference in telling the conscious mind things, and dealing with the automated programs.

(27)

PRE: only . . . NOM: difference, conscious mind; SRV: telling the conscious mind . . . NOM: things; MRI: things; UV: dealing . . . NOM: programs; MRI: programs;

(28)

Because, you see, it's one thing to say, "Only eat fresh food!"

(28)

CE: Because . . . MR: you see . . . MRI: one thing . . . QU: "Only eat fresh food!"

(29)

And then when you walk by a candy counter

(29)

CON: And . . . CE: when . . . MRI: a candy counter . . .

(30)

and your brain goes "brrrhhrrrr," like that,

(30)

CON: and . . . SRV: your brain goes . . . UV: goes . . .

(31)

and all of your unconscious processes have automated the compulsion to eat other things,

(31)

CON: and . . . PRE: all . . . NOM: processes . . . UV: automated . . . NOM: compulsion; MRI: other things; SRV: unconscious processes have automated the compulsion to eat other things;

(32)

so that when that box of Godiva chocolates calls out to you . . .

(32)

CE: when . . . MRI: that box . . . SRV: that box . . . calls out to you

(33)

What's your first name again? (Millie)

(33)

PRE: first, again;

(34)

Millie, when the box of Godiva chocolates calls out to you, Millie and goes: "Millie, you buy a box. You'll only eat one . . . at a time . . . after each other."

(34)

CE: when . . . MRI: the box . . . SRV: box calls out to you . . . UV: goes . . . QU: "Millie . . . other."; PRE: only; MRI: a time . . . PRE: after each other

(35)

And when you walk through the house and the refrigerator calls out and goes: "Millie, there's something in here, and it's just for you, it'll make you feel better."

(35)

CON: And . . . CE: when . . . MRI: the house . . . SRV: the refrigerator calls out . . . UV: goes . . . QU: "Millie . . . better."; MRI: something . . . PRE: just . . . CE: make you feel better; PRE: better; DEL: better than what?

(36)

See, to me like . . . my
microwave talks to me—

(36)

FRA: See, to me like . . .
SRV: my microwave talks
to me;

(36-49)

The microwave metaphor
increases Millie's curiosity in
a humorous way, and indi-
rectly conveys that you
don't have to accept your
present automatic processes,
that you can test and change
them.

(37)

I'm not too schizy—I'm fascinated with it. I will cook
anything in the microwave,

(37)

PRE: too . . . MRI: it . . .
anything . . .

(38)

I put towels, oranges, I'm
just fascinated that it just
goes rrrrrinnnnggggg and
it's hot.

(38)

PRE: just . . . just; MRI: it
. . . UV: goes . . . MRI: it
. . .

(39)

I mean, I can't get over
these things.

(39)

UV: mean . . . can't get
. . . PRE: can't get over
. . . MRI: these things

(40)

How many of you have one
of these things?

(40)

MRI: these things

(41)

What is . . . I mean . . . I'll
stick anything in there.

(41)

FRA: What is . . . I mean
. . . UV: mean . . . stick
. . . MRI: anything

(42)

I don't care what it is, just
to find out, especially when
it said on the outside, "Do
not place aluminum foil in
here," what's the first thing
Richard put in?

(42)

MRI: it . . . PRE: just . . .
UV: find out . . . PRE:
especially . . . CE: when
QU: "Do not . . . here";
PRE: first . . .

(43)

chk-a-chka-chka-chk-a . . .
boy, talk about a light show.

(44)

I got one microwave just to
cook aluminum foil in.

(45)

The one that's built into the
apartment I rented.

(46)

Beautiful light show, it's
great. You turn all the lights
out, throw a TV dinner in
there, leave the aluminum
foil on the top, and you get
a light show and dinner!

(47)

Of course the microwave
doesn't last long, but then I
bring it back and I go, "It's
broken—under warranty."
Ha ha ha ha!

(48)

Fools that you are giving
me something under
warranty.

(49)

Because I'm always afraid
it'll break after the warranty,
so I make sure that it breaks
before the warranty.

(43)

FRA: . . . boy, talk about a
light show; NOM: a light
show; MRI: a light show;

(44)

PRE: one . . . just

(45)

PRE: one . . . MRI: the
apartment

(46)

PRE: all . . . MRI: the aluminum foil; PRE: leave . . .
UV: get . . .

(47)

MRI: the microwave . . .
PRE: long . . . DEL: long
compared to what? CON:
but . . . DEL: back to
where? UV: go . . . QU:
"it's . . . warranty."

(48)

MRI: Fools . . . something
. . . UV: give

(49)

CE: Because . . . PRE:
always . . . MRI: it . . .
PRE: after . . . UV: make
sure . . . MRI: it . . .

(50)

It's like the thing they have when you rent cars where they go, you can take out the insurance and get to wreck the car—for free.

(50)

MRI: It . . . the thing . . . they . . . UV: go . . . MRI: the insurance . . . UV: get to . . . MRI: the car . . .

(50–66)

The car-rental metaphor again amplifies the curiosity state and indirectly conveys that it is possible to challenge automatic processes and act in new, surprising ways.

(51)

I think that is . . . if any of you have children you're going to teach to drive, don't use your own car, man, just give them one of those.

(51)

FRA: I think that is . . . PRE: any . . . just . . . MRI: them . . . those . . .

(52)

Take them out, and have them demolish the thing.

(52)

UV: Take out . . . MRI: them . . . UV: have them demolish . . . MRI: the thing

(53)

I mean, I just think that is one of the best deals, ever.

(53)

UV: mean . . . PRE: just . . . UV: think . . . PRE: the best . . . ever . . . DEL: the best compared to what?

(54)

And it used to be six bucks, they upped it to ten . . . but for ten bucks you can go out and wreck a car,

(54)

CON: And . . . PRE: used to . . . upped it . . . MRI: they . . . CON: but . . . UV: go out . . . wreck . . . MRI: a car

(55)

and I mean, you know, I think . . . I think the Avis people, when they first said . . .

(55)

CON: and . . . UV: mean . . . MR: you know . . . UV: think . . . MRI: the Avis people . . . MRI: it . . . PRE: first . . . FRA: and . . . said."

(56)

and I said, "You mean, you're going to give me insurance and if I pay six bucks I don't have to pay anything if I damage this car?"

(56)

CON: and . . . QU: "You . . . car?" UV: mean . . . MRI: insurance . . . UV: damage . . . CE: if I . . . I don't . . .

(57)

And they'll always look at you and go, "Yeah."

(57)

CON: And . . . MRI: they . . . PRE: always . . . UV: look . . . go . . . QU: "Yeah."

(58)

So I used to take them out and just smack into poles and stuff.

(58)

PRE: just . . . MRI: poles, stuff

(59)

I'd . . . I'd bring 'em back in there'd be nothing there but a chassis and doors kinda hanging on

(59)

MRI: 'em . . . PRE: nothing but . . . MRI: chassis, doors; DEL: hanging on to what?

(60)

and they always go, "What happened?" and I'd go, "I don't know,

(60)

CON: and . . . MRI: they . . . PRE: always . . . UV: go . . . QU: "What happened?" UV: go . . . QU: "I don't know . . . this"

(61)

I parked in front of the 7-11 over there, and when I came out it was like this."

(61)

MRI: the 7-11 . . . it . . . this . . .

(62)

Now, the thing about realizing what's going on, is because, see, the . . . the car-rental people don't think of it that way.

(62)

MRI: the thing . . . PRE: realizing . . . UV: realizing . . . MRI: what . . . FRA: Now the thing about realizing is . . . UV: is going on . . . PRE: what is going on is . . . MRI: the car rental people . . . UV: think . . . MRI: that way

(63)

But if you realize that that's a license to do what you want,

(63)

CON: But . . . CE: if . . . then . . . PRE: realize . . . UV: realize . . . EC: realize . . . MRI: that . . . EC: do what you want

(64)

then the thing that they're counting on is that you have automated processes that say, "Don't wreck this car!"

(64)

MRI: the thing . . . they . . . PRE: the thing is . . . NOM: automated processes . . . SRV: automated processes say . . . QU: "Don't wreck this car."

(65)

Right? It's not in your nature to get into the car and say, "I'm going to wreck this car."

(65)

MRI: It . . . NOM: nature . . . MRI: the car . . . CON: and . . . QU: "I'm . . . car."

Footnote: I use an idiom like rocket scientist because I have used it before. In situations like the client sessions, where I'm coming in cold, I always define idiomatic speech when I use it. In this seminar I had already talked about how you don't have to be a rocket scientist to be a great salesman, you just have to keep your eyes open.

(66)

Except every once in a while.

(66)

PRE: Except . . . MRI: a while . . .

(67)

But you have automated processes that tell you to do things like not eat and follow those four prin . . . those four principles aren't news to you, are they?

(67)

CON: But . . . MR: you have . . . NOM: automated processes . . . SRV: automated processes tell you . . . MRI: things . . . EC: follow . . . NOM: principles . . . news . . .

(67-69)

I want to make sure that she knows the basic principles, although I don't want her just to know them, I want her to use them.

(68)

You eat fresh food, you eat at regular intervals, you exercise a little bit, and you eat stuff that's good for you, and you don't eat too much of it.

(68)

EC: eat fresh food, eat at regular intervals, exercise a little bit . . . eat stuff that's good for you; PRE: fresh . . . regular . . . little bit . . . good . . . DEL: how fresh, how regular, little bit for who, good in what way? MRI: stuff . . . CON: and . . . EC: don't eat too much . . . PRE: too . . . MR: it

(69)

And you don't need to be a rocket scientist to know that.

(69)

CON: And . . . PRE: rocket scientist; MRI: rocket scientist; UV: know . . . MRI: that

(70)

You have to be a rocket scientist to do it. Right!

(70)

PRE: rocket scientist; MRI: rocket scientist; UV: do . . . MRI: it . . .

(70-71)

In other words, you don't have to be smart to figure out you need to do it, you have to be smart enough to do it. And to do it now.

(71)

Because rocket scientists
have no conscious minds.
It's your conscious mi . . .

(71)

CE: Because . . . NOM:
conscious minds . . . MRI:
It . . .

(72)

He, he, you can't laugh,
you have to leave the room,
okay? Or you must go into
trance, too.

(72)

EC: leave the room . . .
NOM: trance; PRE: too
. . .

(72)

Somebody walked into the
room and started laughing
and I just utilize it, because I
didn't want to disrupt the
people who were there.
Mention anything that happens when you're doing
trance work with people.
Utilize every noise that
occurs, don't ignore any
sound. Anything that breaks
into your consciousness is
probably going to break
into theirs, and then they
start thinking instead of
responding.

(73)

Now what we're gonna do
is we're gonna have a little
talk with your unconscious.

(73)

PRE: what . . . is . . . PRE:
little . . . NOM: talk; SRV:
talk with your unconscious;
NOM: unconscious

(74)

Because, see, your uncon-
scious knows how to con-
trol compulsions because
you know what weight you
would like to be, right?

(74)

CE: Because . . . NOM:
unconscious; UV: knows
. . . NOM: compulsions;
CE: because . . . MR: you
know . . . UV: know . . .
NOM: weight

(75)

Okay, now can you make a
picture in your mind of
where you would like to be,
clear, focused, rich image;

(75)

CP: can you make a picture
. . . NOM: mind; DEL: like
to be when, for what pur-
pose? PRE: clear, focused,
rich

(76)

Now, what I want you to
do is to keep looking at that
image;

(76)

PRE: keep . . . MRI: that
. . . NOM: image

(77)

I'll tell you when to open
your eyes. You'll know
You'll have no doubt. You
won't need an interpreter.

(77)

CE: when . . . UV: know
. . . DEL: know what?
NOM: doubt; DEL: no
doubt about what? MRI:
interpreter; DEL: no interpreter for what?

(78)

Okay, and don't be ner-
vous, be terrified of not getting what you want.

(78)

CON: and . . . UV: be . . .
be . . .

(78)

Reframe: "Don't be ner-
vous, be terrified of not getting what you want."

Instead of reframing all the
possible objections clients
may have to a desired
change (i.e., "If I lose
weight, men will be
approaching me . . . " etc.)
this is a way of telling them
they don't need to be afraid
of getting what they want
and they need to learn to
decide what makes them
happy.

(79)

Because if you don't learn
to control your own life and
your own happiness,
because it's not just about
whether you lose 10 pounds
or gain 10 pounds,

(79)

CE: Because . . . PRE:
learn . . . UV: learn, control
. . . NOM: life, happiness;
CE: because . . . PRE: just
. . . lose . . . gain . . . UV:
lose, gain

(79-80)

The use of a higher nomi-
nalization (happiness)
reduces the importance of
weight loss as a goal and
reorients Millie in a more
useful direction.

(80)

it's about at any moment in time changing your ability to make a decision and stick to it.

(80)

MRI: it . . . UV: changing . . . NOM: ability EC: make a decision . . . NOM: decision; UV: stick to it; EC: stick to it . . . MRI: it

(81)

Because if you quit smoking, gain weight, then you start dieting and you smoke, you're playing ping-pong with your life.

(81)

CE: Because if . . . then; UV: quit . . . gain . . . start . . . NOM: life

(81)

This emphasizes the presupposition that she is making the decisions to do it and thus implies that she can decide to do it differently.

(82)

Now, if you want to smoke, smoke. If you want to eat and be fat, eat and be fat.

(82)

CE: if . . . if . . . DEL: smoke what? eat what? how fat?

(82-91)

Cause-effect for failed diets in the past that provides a reason why things are going to be different in the future, because otherwise she can sabotage the work by reinstalling the problem. ("Is this going to work, or is it the same as what I've tried before?").

(83)

But if you don't want to you shouldn't have to, as soon as you learn to control the unconscious portions of your mind.

(83)

CON: But . . . DEL: shouldn't . . . CE: as soon as . . . PRE: learn . . . UV: learn, control; NOM: unconscious portions; PRE: unconscious . . . NOM: mind

(84)

Because the behaviors you learned, you learned only because you were born and grew up.

(84)

CE: Because . . . MRI: the behaviors . . . UV: learned . . . PRE: learned . . . only . . . CE: because . . .

(85)

If you weren't born and you didn't grow up you wouldn't have problems.

(85)

CE: If . . . NOM: problems; MRI: problems

(86)

But since you did, you learned to do things, everything from walking and talking,

(86)

IC: But since . . . DEL: did what? PRE: learned . . . UV: learned . . . UV: do . . . NOM: things; MRI: things; PRE: everything . . .

(87)

having speech and language, learning to make clear images in your mind, learning to read and write, learning to do a whole plethora of things;

(87)

PRE: having . . . learning . . . EC: make clear images . . . NOM: mind . . . PRE: learning . . . learning . . . UV: do . . . MRI: a whole plethora of things; NOM: plethora, things

(88)

and some of them are so automatic, they're as automatic as a handshake,

(88)

CON: and . . . PRE: some . . . MRI: some, them; PRE: so . . . as . . . as . . .

(88)

Induces arm catalepsy and utilizes hand movement as proof for the previously made statements.

(89)

and somebody walks up and extends their hand to you, your hand lifts up like that to shake their hand,

(89)

CON: and . . . MRI: somebody . . . PRE: extends . . . MRI: their . . . PRE: lifts up . . .

(90)

and it doesn't take any knowledge, no understanding to do it.

(90)

CON: and . . . MRI: it . . . NOM: knowledge, understanding; UV: do . . . EC: do it

(91)

But your unconscious mind knows how to do it, in such a way that that learning stays with you for the rest of your life.

(91)

CON: But . . . NOM: unconscious mind; SRV: your unconscious mind knows; MR: knows . . . PRE: knows . . . UV: knows . . . PHON. AMB.: knows–nose; UV: do; MRI: it; EC: do it; MRI: that learning; NOM: learning; PRE: stays . . . NOM: rest, life

(92)

Now, what I want you to do is to begin a new learn-ing, a new understanding such that, at the uncon-scious level, you can begin to make changes that will last and satisfy you and delight you.

(92)

PRE: what . . . is . . . UV: do . . . begin . . . PRE: new . . . NOM: learning, understanding, unconscious level; PRE: begin . . . UV: begin . . . make . . . NOM: changes . . . MRI: changes; DEL: last . . . satisfy . . . delight . . .

(92-94)

Review of successful past automatic programs supports the presupposition that she already knows how to do it.

(93)

I want your conscious mind now to begin to run memo-ries of times and places where you've eaten right and dealt with food in an intelligent and a productive manner.

(93)

NOM: conscious mind; PRE: begin . . . UV: run memories . . . NOM: memories, times, places; MRI: memories, times, places; DEL: right for what? UV: dealt with food . . .

(94)

And keep those images, bits and pieces of past times that you haven't learned, that haven't stayed with you, yet, in just the way you want it

(94)

CON: And . . . PRE: keep those images . . . MRI: bits and pieces; NOM: times; MRI: that; PRE: haven't learned; MRI: that; PRE: haven't stayed . . . yet . . . MRI: it

(95)

and allow me to speak privately with parts of you that understand only the things that count.

(95)

CON: and . . . CP: allow me . . . SRV: speak with parts of you . . . parts that understand . . . PRE: only . . . NOM: things; MRI: things

(96)

Because what I want your unconscious to do is allow this hand to slowly go down, only at the rate that your other hand begins to lift up, involuntarily.

(96)

CE: Because . . . PRE: what . . . is . . . NOM: unconscious . . . UV: do; PRE: allow . . . slowly . . . only . . . begins . . . involuntarily

(97)

That's right, very slowly now, and unconsciously,

(97)

MRI: That's; DEL: right for whom? PRE: very slowly . . . unconsciously

(97-103)

Suggestion that the automatic processes for weight control are being readjusted.

(98)

and no faster than your unconscious begins to make shifts that will stay with you for the rest of your life.

(98)

CON: and . . . PRE: no faster . . . NOM: unconscious; PRE: begins . . . UV: begins, make; MRI: shifts; PRE: stay . . . NOM: rest, life

(99)

that slowly begin to take that furnace inside and turn up the temperature

(99)

PRE: slowly . . . begin . . . take . . . UV: begin, take; EC: begin . . . take . . . SRV: furnace inside; PRE: turn up; EC: turn up; NOM: temperature

(100)

and turn up the burning sensation and digestion of food

(100)

CON: and . . . PRE: turn up . . . EC: turn up . . . NOM: sensation, digestion

(101)

in such a way that while your health remains perfect, in fact, while you get healthier, you begin to dissipate unwanted fat.

(101)

IC: while . . . PRE: remains . . . UV: remains; IC: while . . . UV: get; EC: get healthier; PRE: begin; EC: begin; PRE: dissipate . . .

(102)

Because your unconscious knows how to set a weight in the middle, so that you can float a little bit up, and way down from,

(102)

EC: Because . . . NOM: unconscious; MR: knows; UV: knows; IC: so that . . . PRE: a little bit up, way down

(103)

and it has just set it somewhere that's not satisfactory to you.

(103)

CON: and . . . MRI: it . . . PRE: just . . . UV: set it . . . MRI: somewhere; DEL: not satisfactory

(104)

It's now time to turn back the pages of time,

(104)

MRI: It; NOM: time; DEL: time for whom? PRE: turn back . . . SRV: turn back the pages of time;

(104-106)

Pacing and reorientation of past compulsions. Installation of a decision point.

(105)

and let your unconscious readjust the compulsions that are inside you,

(105)

CON: and . . . UV: let . . . NOM: unconscious; PRE: readjust; NOM: compulsions; MRI: the compulsions

(106)

such that, when you look at food you know is not the best food for you to eat, your unconscious is going to say, "Not today."

(106)

CE: when; MR: you know; PRE: the best; DEL; the best; NOM: unconscious; SRV: your unconscious is going to say; QU: "Not today."

(107)

And when you start to eat at a time that you know is not the right time,

(107)

CON: And; CE: when . . . PRE: start . . . MRI: a time; NOM: time; MR: you know; PRE: right . . . DEL: right for who?

(107-109)

Pacing and reorientation of past compulsions. Installation of a new strategy.

(108)

your unconscious will send a message to you that will make you feel in your whole self, "Not now,"

(108)

NOM: unconscious; SRV: unconscious will send a message; NOM: message; MRI: message; PRE: whole; NOM: self; QU: "Not now"

(109)

such that instead of your world revolving around a struggle with food, it begins to become more comfortable for you to make the decisions that are the right decisions that will begin to change your relationship to food,

(109)

NOM: world; PRE: instead; NOM: struggle; PRE: begins, become, more; UV: begins . . . become . . . EC: make the decisions; UV: make; NOM: decisions; MRI: decisions; DEL: right for what? MRI: that; PRE: begin; UV: begin; PRE: change; UV: change; DEL: change; NOM: relationship

(110)

in such a way that as your compulsion to eat the wrong food diminishes, your pleasure and lust for life will increase proportionally, as your hands are moving now.

(110)

IC: as . . . as; NOM: compulsion; DEL: wrong for what? PRE: diminishes . . . NOM: pleasure, lust, life; PRE: increase, proportionally

(110-115)

"Getting stuck in the process" builds a compulsion in a new direction.

(111)

I want your left hand to slowly begin to feel attracted to your face,

(111)

PRE: slowly; SRV: hand to begin feel attracted; PRE: begin; DEL: feel attracted

(112)

almost as if there's a rubber
band between your hand
and your nose such that it
grows stronger and stronger,

(112)

PRE: almost as . . . MRI:
it; PRE: grows stronger and
stronger

(113)

but I want you to get stuck
in the process.

(113)

CON: but; EC: get stuck;
UV: get stuck; NOM: pro-
cess

(114)

I want it to be difficult, if
not near-impossible, and I
want you to begin to try in
vain to touch your face.

(114)

PRE: difficult; DEL: difficult for whom? PRE:
impossible; DEL: impossible
for whom? PRE: begin;
UV: begin; EC: begin; UV:
try; EC: try; PRE: in vain;
PRE: touch; UV: touch

(115)

And while that attraction
grows stronger, and as strong
as the attraction to what it is
that you want to learn, I
want you to feel that struggle in your arm growing.

(115)

CON: And . . . IC: while
. . . MRI: that attraction;
NOM: attraction; PRE:
grows . . . stronger . . . as
strong . . . MRI: it; PRE:
what . . . is . . . learn . . .
UV: learn; EC: feel that
struggle; MRI: that struggle;
NOM: struggle; PRE:
growing; UV: growing

(116)

Because if that struggle
grows and intensifies, I want
your unconscious to make
all the necessary adjustments
for you at the unconscious
level

(116)

CE: Because; MRI: that
struggle; PRE: grows, inten-
sifies; NOM: unconscious;
EC: make the adjustments;
SRV: unconscious makes
adjustments; PRE: all . . .
DEL: necessary for what?
NOM: unconscious level

(116-118)

Utilization of the physical
struggle she experiences as
evidence for adjustments on
the unconscious level.

(117)

to begin to get exactly what
you want, to change the
feelings you have about
food,

(117)

PRE: begin; UV: begin;
EC: get exactly what you
want; PRE: exactly; MRI:
what . . . EC: change the
feelings; UV: change;
NOM: feelings; MRI:
feelings

(118)

and to change your metabolism in a way that allows you
to keep your weight down
to where you want to.

(118)

CON: and . . . PRE:
change; UV: change;
NOM: metabolism; PRE:
keep, down

(119)

And as that struggle grows
more and more intense, as
the attraction grows
stronger at the unconscious
level,

(119)

CON: And; IC: as; MRI:
that struggle; NOM: struggle; PRE: grows, more and
more intense; NOM: attraction; PRE: grows stronger;
NOM: unconscious level;
MRI: the unconscious level;

(119-124)

Amplification of the com-
pulsion that leads to a positive feeling.

(120)

you'll be making changes
now, changes that will stay
with you for the rest of your
life.

(120)

NOM: changes, changes;
PRE: stay; NOM: rest, life

(121)

And as that struggle intensifies, I want your hand to
proceed up towards your
face,

(121)

CON: And; IC: as . . .
MRI: that struggle; NOM:
struggle; PRE: intensifies,
proceed, up

(122)

at the rate that your unconscious has thoroughly made
all the adjustments to allow
you to have the choice that
you want, and need, for
yourself and no faster,

(122)

NOM: unconscious; PRE:
thoroughly, all; NOM:
adjustments; MRI: adjust-
ments; EC: have the choice;
PRE: no faster

(123)

that's right, such that when
your hand does touch your
face in a moment, then, and
only then, you'll feel an
explosion of confidence and
vigor spread throughout
your entire body,

(123)

MRI: that; DEL: right for
who? CE: when; PRE:
only; NOM: explosion,
confidence, vigor; SRV:
feel an explosion spread
throughout your body

(124)

Now, that's right.

(124)

MRI: that's; DEL: right for
who/what?

(125)

And enjoy that feeling, and
realize that every time you
make the right choice,
you're going to have that
feeling,

(125)

CON: And; PRE: enjoy;
UV: enjoy; MRI: that;
NOM: feeling; PRE: real-
ize; UV: realize; PRE: every
time; CE: make the right
choice, have that feeling;
EC: make the right choice;
UV: make; DEL: right for
who/what? NOM: choice;
EC: have that feeling; MRI:
that; NOM: feeling

(126)

and it's going to intensify and intensify and spread, and you're going to enjoy the process because each good choice you make is going to feel that wonderful.

(126)

CON: and; MRI: it; PRE: intensify and intensify; EC: intensify, spread; CON: and . . . and; PRE: enjoy; UV: enjoy; EC: enjoy; NOM: process; MRI: the process; CE: because . . . DEL: good for who/what? NOM: choice; EC: feel that wonderful; MRI: that wonderful

(127)

And it will take all the pleasures in your life and intensify them tenfold.

(127)

CON: And; MRI: it; UV: take; PRE: take all; EC: take the pleasures; NOM: pleasures; MRI: pleasures; EC: intensify; MRI: them

(127-133)

Amplification of the positive feeling.

(128)

That's right. There you go . . . Enjoying it more.

(128)

MRI: That's; DEL: right; MRI: There; PRE: enjoying . . . MRI: it; PRE: more; Fragment: enjoying it more;

(129)

Because your unconscious leads you through life and controls your neurology

(129)

CE: Because . . . NOM: unconscious; UV: leads; NOM: life; SRV: your unconscious leads you through life; UV: controls; NOM: neurology;

(130)

in such a way, that to help
you make choices, it doesn't
have the values about what
choices are good or bad, but
it's always more than willing
to cooperate.

(130)

PRE: help; UV: make;
NOM: choices; MRI: it;
NOM: values; MRI: values;
NOM: choices; MRI:
choices; DEL: good or bad
for who/what? CON: but;
MRI: it; PRE: always,
more; UV: cooperate; DEL:
cooperate on what?

(131)

Now your unconscious
knows just how to spread
this feeling;

(131)

NOM: unconscious; MR:
unconscious knows; UV:
knows; PRE: knows;
PHON.AMB.: knows-nose;
PRE: just; SRV: spread the
feeling; NOM: feeling

(132)

it can do it right now.
There it comes.

(132)

MRI: it; UV: do; MRI: it;
PRE: right now . . .

(133)

And feel that feeling spread
throughout your body, and
know you'd rather feel
good.

(133)

CON: And . . . PRE: feel;
EC: feel; MRI: that; NOM:
feeling; PRE: spread; UV:
spread; CON: and . . .
PRE: know; UV: know;
DEL: rather than what? EC:
feel good

(134)

Now, your unconscious can
remember a time when you
felt so full, you couldn't eat
another bite.

(134)

NOM: unconscious; PRE:
remember: MRI: a time

(134-140)

Induction of a sensation of
fullness.

Installation of a new strategy: Decide how much to
eat-feel full-stop eating-pos-
itive feeling.

Introduction of the notion
of unconscious learning.

(135)

And I want a memory such as that to fill you right now, so much so that you couldn't think of eating another bite.

(135)

CON: And; NOM: memory; MRI: memory, that; SRV: I want a memory to fill you; UV: fill; think; PRE: another

(136)

And I want your unconscious to give you this feeling every time you should stop eating.

(136)

CON: And; NOM: unconscious; UV: give; NOM: feeling; MRI: this feeling; PRE: every; NOM: time; DEL: should in order to do what?

(137)

And when you look at a plate of food at the beginning of a meal I want your conscious and unconscious mind to decide together how much of it you should eat.

(137)

CON: And; CE: when . . . EC: look; MRI: a plate of food, a meal; NOM: conscious and unconscious mind; SRV: conscious and unconscious mind to decide together; MRI: it; DEL: should in order to do what?

(138)

And at the moment you have eaten that much, I want you to get this feeling of fullness and stop eating,

(138)

CON: And; MRI: the moment . . . that much . . . EC: get this feeling; MRI: this feeling; NOM: feeling, fullness; EC: stop eating

(139)

and suddenly start feeling good, because the minute you make the right choice, that's what happens.

(139)

CON: and . . . PRE: suddenly . . . start . . . CE: because . . . DEL: right for who/what? NOM: choice; MRI: that; UV: happens

(140)

That's right, and that's the power of unconscious learning.

(140)

MRI: that's; DEL: right; CON: and; MRI: that's; NOM: power; MRI: power; NOM: unconscious learning

(141)

You've always really learned unconsciously.

(141)

PRE: always, really, learned; UV: learned; PRE: unconsciously

(141-143)

The alphabet metaphor links the new direction to already-accomplished learnings and builds confidence in her ability t) learn unconsciously.

(142)

When you learned the letters of the alphabet, you didn't realize they make up a whole domain of reading and writing that will stay with you forever.

(142)

PRE: you learned, didn't realize: UV: realize; MRI: they; NOM: domain, reading, writing; PRE: stay

(143)

You didn't realize how many ways you could use it.

(143)

PRE: realize; UV: realize; PRE: many; NOM: ways; UV: use; MRI: it

(144)

But these are the building blocks of having the choices you want,

(144)

CON: But; MRI: these; NOM: choices; MRI: choices; DEL: want for what?

(145)

knowing how to feel full, and knowing what happens if you make the right choice, now.

(145)

PRE: knowing; UV: knowing; EC: feel full; PRE: knowing; UV: knowing, happens, make; DEL: right for who/what? NOM: choice

(146)

Your unconscious is learning a lot. That's right.

(146)

NOM: unconscious; PRE: learning; UV: learning; PRE: a lot; MRI: a lot; That's; DEL: right for who/what?

(147)

And it's showing you and convincing you how powerful that learning is.

(147)

CON: And; MRI: it's; PRE: showing, convincing; UV: showing, convincing; MRI: that learning; PRE: learning; NOM: learning

(148)

So I want you to let your hand move away from your mouth for a change,

(148)

CE: So . . . PRE: move away, for a change

(148-153)

Anchors the positive feeling to the decision not to eat or smoke.

(149)

that's right, and that feels awfully good, doesn't it?

(149)

MRI: that's; DEL: right for who/what? CON: and; MRI: that; PRE: awfully; DEL: awfully good for who/what?

(150)

Because each time your hand doesn't go to your mouth, and you make that choice, you're going to get that good feeling.

(150)

CE: Because; PRE: each; NOM: time; CON: and; EC: make that choice; NOM: choice; MRI: that choice; UV: get; MRI: that; DEL: good for who/what? NOM: feeling

(151)

That's right. You don't need to smoke it, and you don't need to swallow it, you just need to enjoy it—

(151)

MRI: that's; DEL: right for who/what? MRI: it; CON: and; MRI: it; PRE: just, enjoy; UV: enjoy; MRI: it

(152)

it's Richard's hedonistic way of changing the problem into a pleasant distraction—

(152)

MRI: it's; UV: changing; MRI: the problem; NOM: problem, distraction; MRI: distraction

(153)

and to focus that energy on something that would be even more useful.

(153)

CON: and; EC: focus; UV: focus; MRI: that energy; NOM: energy; MRI: something, that; PRE: even more

(154)

And I want you to drop, now, even deeper and deeper into a trance

(154)

CON: And; EC: drop; DEL: drop; PRE: even deeper and deeper; NOM: trance; MRI: trance

(154-157)

Deepens trance.

(155)

and let your unconscious be your guide, and show you the ways (waves)

(155)

CON: and; NOM: unconscious; DEL: guide for what? CON: and; PRE: show; UV: show; MRI: the ways; PHON.AMB. : ways-waves;

(156)

and you feel yourself float down a little bit, up a little bit,

(156)

CON: and; EC: feel . . . float down; PRE: float down, a little bit, up a little bit

(157)

and while you continue to float down you're learning even more,

(157)

CON: and; IC: while; PRE: continue; EC: float; PRE: down, learning; UV: learning; PRE: even more

(158)

and your unconscious is now making changes to adjust your metabolic furnace

(158)

CON: and; NOM: unconscious; SRV: unconscious is making changes; UV: making changes; MRI: changes; DEL: making changes; EC: adjust; UV: adjust; SRV: unconscious adjusts metabolic furnace

(158-163)

Reorientation of the past feeling of hunger.

(159)

to replace the feeling of hunger as necessary in the past, with a smaller amount of hunger only when it's appropriate to eat,

(159)

PRE: replace; UV: replace; NOM: feeling, hunger; MRI: the feeling of hunger; DEL: necessary for who/what? MRI: in the past; NOM: past; PRE: smaller; NOM: amount, hunger; PRE: only; DEL: appropriate for who/what?

(160)

by taking all those extra feelings and turning them into wanton pleasure,

(160)

CE: by . . . PRE: taking; UV: taking; PRE: all; MRI: those; NOM: feelings; PRE: turning; UV: turning; MRI: them; NOM: pleasure

(161)

and a desire to be more energetic, to walk up stairs and exercise in whatever way gives you the greatest pleasure, no matter what comes to mind.

(161)

CON: and; MRI: a desire; NOM: desire; PRE: more; EC: be more energetic . . . walk . . . MRI: stairs; EC: exercise; MRI: whatever way; PRE: gives you; UV: gives you; PRE: greatest; NOM: pleasure; MRI: pleasure

(162)

That's right. Burning calories at every moment,

(162)

MRI: That's; DEL: right for
who/what? SYN.AMB. :
Burning calories; MRI:
calories; NOM: calories;
PRE: every; NOM:
moment; MRI: moment

(163)

and while you drift down
deeper I want your uncon-
scious to realize it's respon-
sible and to take responsibility for making these changes
last and stay with you.

(163)

CON: and; IC: while;
PRE: drift; EC: drift down;
PRE: deeper; NOM:
unconscious; PRE: realize;
UV: realize; DEL: responsi-
ble for what? PRE: take;
UV: take; NOM: responsi-
bility; MRI: responsibility,
these changes; NOM:
changes; UV: making these
changes; PRE: last, stay;
UV: last, stay

(164)

Because the process of taking building blocks and
making them into new
compulsions, more useful
ways of supplementing your
behavior,

(164)

CE: Because . . . NOM:
process; MRI: process;
PRE: taking; UV: taking;
MRI: building blocks;
CON: and; PRE: making;
UV: making; MRI: them;
PRE: new; NOM: compul-
sions; MRI: compulsions;
PRE: more; NOM: ways;
MRI: ways; PRE: supple-
menting; UV: supplement-
ing; NOM: behavior

(164-165)

Refers back to the alphabet
metaphor and reinduces the
state of confidence in her
ability to learn unconsciously. Establishes the new compulsions as the foundations
for satisfying behaviors.

(165)

and utilizing them in such a
way to build a solid founda-
tion for behaving in a way
that satisfies you.

(165)

CON: and . . . PRE: utilizing; UV: utilizing; MRI:
them, such a way; EC: build
. . . UV: build; MRI: foun-
dation; NOM: way; MRI:
way

(166)

So I want you now to begin to see, off into your own future, tomorrow, two weeks from now,

(166)

PRE: begin, see; EC: see . . . NOM: future

(166-172)

Future-paces falling off the diet and starting it again.

(167)

and I want you to see yourself sticking diligently to your diet, and then failing utterly in five days,

(167)

CON: and . . . PRE: see . . . EC: see yourself; PRE: sticking; UV: sticking; PRE: diligently; CON: and; MRI: then; PRE: utterly

(168)

and then going back on your diet, and then failing utterly once in two weeks.

(168)

CON: and . . . MRI: then . . . PRE: going back . . . UV: going back . . . NOM: diet; CON: and . . . MRI: then . . . PRE: utterly

(169)

And then go six months into your future, and make another mistake,

(169)

CON: And . . . SRV: go six months into your future; UV: go into your future; CON: and . . . PRE: another; UV: make; NOM: mistake

(170)

and then as you look into the future, you'll realize the whole time you got thinner and thinner

(170)

CON: and; IC: as . . . EC: look into the future; NOM: future; PRE: realize; UV: realize; PRE: thinner and thinner; DEL thinner and who/what?

(171)

because instead of going
from one diet to another, to
another, you realize if you
make a mistake you just go
back, and continue.

(171)

CE: because; PRE: instead;
UV: going; NOM: diet;
MRI: one diet . . . PRE:
realize; UV: realize; CE: if
. . . UV: make a mistake;
NOM: mistake; MRI: mis-
take; PRE: just . . . go back
. . . UV: go back, continue;
PRE: continue; UV: con-
tinue; DEL: continue what?

(172)

And you don't give yourself
a bad time, you just realize
that if it didn't feel as good
as it was supposed to, it's
not worth doing again.

(172)

CON: And . . . PRE: just,
realize; UV: realize; CE: if;
MRI: it; EC: feel good;
PRE: as . . . as . . . MRI: it
. . . DEL: supposed to;
MRI: it; DEL: not worth;
PRE: again

(173)

Instead you go back to what
really feels good and do it a
lot more.

(173)

PRE: Instead, go back; UV:
go back; MRI: what; PRE:
really; DEL: feels good in
what way? CON: and; EC:
do it; PRE: a lot more;
DEL: a lot more compared
to what?

(174)

Now, I want your uncon-
scious to take that feeling
you had before, and multiply it by ten,

(174)

NOM: unconscious; PRE:
take; UV: take; MRI: that;
NOM: feeling; CON: and;
SRV: multiply a feeling;

(175)

just to remind you that
when you see yourself in
your mind in the future
going back on your diet, I
want to give you that good
feeling, now—

(175)

PRE: just, remind; CE:
when . . . EC: see yourself;
NOM: mind, future; PRE:
going back; UV: going
back; NOM: diet; PRE:
give you, now; MRI: that
good feeling; NOM: feeling

(176)

that's right, there you go—

(176)

MRI: that's; DEL: right for
who/what? UV: go

(177)

and to realize how good it
feels to know that you can
make a mistake and enjoy
fixing it.

(177)

CON: and; PRE: realize;
UV: realize; MRI: it; UV:
know; PRE: know; UV:
make; NOM: mistake;
MRI: a mistake; PRE:
enjoy; UV: enjoy, fixing;
MRI: it

(177-179)

Prevents the reoccurrence of
old responses to falling off
the diet and sets a new
direction for these situations.

(178)

There you go.

(178)

UV: go

(179)

Because the process of
learning doesn't require perfection, only tenacity.

(179)

CE: Because; NOM: pro-
cess, learning, perfection;
MRI: process, learning, perfection; PRE: only; NOM:
tenacity

(180)

Now, what I want your
unconscious mind to do is
to slowly begin to involuntarily lift this hand up

(180)

PRE: what . . . is . . .
NOM: unconscious mind;
UV: do; PRE: slowly,
begin; UV: begin; PRE:
involuntarily, lift up

(180-187)

Utilization of the hand
movement as evidence for
the unconscious adopting
the new responses in the
future.

(181)

and to make all the adjustments and all the changes
that it needs to guarantee
that there will be no more
waiting around for a solution to this problem.

(181)

CON: and; EC: make all
the adjustments; PRE: all;
NOM: adjustments; MRI:
adjustments; UV: make;
CON: and; PRE: all;
NOM: changes; MRI:
changes, it; UV: needs,
guarantee; PRE: no more;
NOM: solution, problem;
MRI: a solution, this
problem

(182)

That's right, honest unconscious movement,

(182)

MRI: That's; DEL: right for
who/what? PRE: honest,
unconscious; FRA: honest,
unconscious movement

(183)

and when your unconscious
is thoroughly ready to take
full responsibility for making
sure that these changes are
there in the days and weeks
ahead,

(183)

CON: and; CE: when . . .
NOM: unconscious; PRE:
thoroughly . . . take; UV:
take; PRE: full; NOM:
responsibility; MRI: responsibility; PRE: making sure;
UV: making sure; MRI:
these changes; NOM:
changes

(184)

so that every right choice
feels intense pleasure,

(184)

PRE: every; DEL: right for
who/what? NOM: choice;
MRI: choice; PRE: intense;
NOM: pleasure; MRI: plea-
sure; SRV: every right
choice feels intense pleasure

(185)

and every mistake will be
inconsequential, and does
not get dwelled upon.

(185)

CON: and; PRE: every;
NOM: mistake; DEL:
inconsequential; CON: and
. . . UV: dwelled upon

(186)

Then, and only then, will
your hand be once again
touching your face.

(186)

CE: Then . . . PRE: only,
once again; UV: touching

(187)

But this time it will be
empty and ready to feel
good in a new way.

(187)

CON: But; PRE: this time;
MRI: it; EC: feel good;
UV: feel good; PRE: in a
new way; MRI: in a new
way

(188)

Now I want you to take
your time so that your
unconscious thoroughly
does this with completeness
and intensity,

(188)

PRE: take; UV: take;
NOM: time; MRI: time;
IC: so that . . . NOM:
unconscious; PRE: thor-
oughly; PRE: with com-
pleteness and intensity;
NOM: completeness and
intensity; MRI: complete-
ness, intensity

(188-191)

Anchors trance state.

(189)

so that anytime in the future
if it begins to become a
problem, you just simply sit
down in your chair

(189)

IC: so that . . . MRI: any-
time; NOM: future; MRI:
it; PRE: begins, become;
NOM: problem; MRI:
problem; PRE: just, simply;
EC: sit down; MRI: chair

(190)

and remember how to
touch your face in just this
way.

(190)

CON: and; PRE: remem-
ber; EC: remember; UV:
remember; PRE: just;
NOM: way; MRI: this way

(191)

That's right, there you go,
and feel good.

(191)

MRI: That's; DEL: right for
who/what? UV: go; EC:
feel good; UV: feel good

(192)

Now, very slowly, at your own rate of speed,

(192)

PRE: very slowly, at your own rate of speed; NOM: rate, speed

(192-201)

Induction of "waking-up" state.

(193)

I want you to realize that if I touch you like this, you can go right back into a trance anytime you need to,

(193)

PRE: realize; UV: realize; CE: if . . . UV: go right back; PRE: right back; NOM: trance; PRE: any-time

(194)

and, of course you know what this means.

(194)

CON: and . . . PRE: of course . . . MR: you know; PRE: you know; UV: know; MRI: this; PRE: means; UV: means

(195)

That's right. And remember it and use it wisely.

(195)

MRI: That's; DEL: right for who/what?

(196)

Now, take a few moments at your own rate of speed,

(196)

PRE: take; UV: take; MRI: a few; NOM: moments; NOM: rate, speed; PRE: at your own rate of speed

(197)

and I want you to slowly float out of the trance so that I can speak to the rest of you,

(197)

CON: and . . . PRE: slow-ly, float out; NOM: trance; MRI: the trance; IC: so that . . . DEL: speak about what? NOM: rest; MRI: the rest of you . . .

(198)

take your own time, there is no hurry,

(198)

EC: take your own time; PRE: take; UV: take; NOM: time; NOM: hurry

(199)

and feel yourself come up, (louder) alert, refreshed, and ready for lust, life.

(199)

CON: and . . . EC: feel . . . PRE: feel; PRE: come up; PRE: alert, refreshed, ready; NOM: lust, life; MRI: lust, life

(200)

Hello, how do you feel?

Millie: I feel great.

Richard: Good, I'm hungry now. How about you?

(Laughter)

No? Well, life is like that sometimes, you just get it your way,

(200)

NOM: hungry, life; MRI: life, that, sometimes; PRE: just; UV: get; MRI: it; NOM: way

(201)

and there is nothing you can do about it. What can I say? What do you all look so blurry-eyed for? I was talking to her.

(201)

CON: and . . . UV: do; MRI: it; PRE: all . . . so . . .

Appendix

The Milton Model

A. CASUAL MODELING PROCESSES

Within the language we use in making sense of our experience, we often try to "explain" the connections between different parts of our model of the world in casual terms We employ the tems of natural language and typically assume a necessary connection between these parts of our experience.

Such explanations are often absurd in that they attempt to reduce the complex circumstances involved in some event to a simple, often single "cause." In the context of hypnosis however, where one of the objectives is, initially, to pace and then lead the client's experience, this process has a positive value. The hypnotist can make use of it to assist the client in achieving the desired state of trance. [Specifically, the hypnotist can make casual connections between verifiable portions of the client's experience and the desired behavior. The strength of the connection varies from simple co-occurrence to one of necessity.]

1. Conjunctions

Use of the connectives "and," "but" (i.e., "and not"). These represent the weakest form of linkage.

"You can look at me and feel an increasing sense of curiosity."

"You can sometimes seem confused, but continue to learn unconsciously."

2. Implied causative

Use of the connectives "as," "while," "during," "before," "after," etcetera

"Since you are here, you can easily learn in new and different ways."

"As you think of new solutions, you can go even deeper into a trance."

3. Cause-effect

Use of predicates that express a necessary connection between portions of the speaker's experience, such as "make," "cause," "force," "require," "because," "if . . . then," etc.

"Using these language patterns will make you a better hypnotist."

"You won't have the same problem again, because now you know what to do."

B. MIND-READING

This is a modeling process closely related to casual modeling. Mind-reading statements are statements in which one person claims to know the thoughts and feelings of another person, without specifying the process by which he came to that information. They are useful in pacing and leading the client.

"You must be wondering what this means."

"You will soon experience an even deeper sense of comfort."

C. TRANSDERIVATIONAL PHENOMENA

Transderivation refers to the process the listener goes through to make meaning. Upon hearing a surface structure and recovering its associated deep structure which has little or no obvious meaning relationship to the listener's ongoing experience, the listener activates additional meaning recovery process which develop meanings, and are available to the unconscious portion of the client's mind but not to the conscious portion. From this set the client will select the meaning that is most relevant to his ongoing experience. The forms of surface structure that activate transderivational search are:

1. Generalized Referential Index

Sentences with noun phrases with no reference to client's experience allow him full access to the transderivational search process.

"Certain sensations in your hand will increase."

"People can learn to get much more enjoyment out of their lives."

2. Unspecified Verbs

The use of unspecified verbs enables you to pace the client, as it maximizes the likelihood of the statement fitting his experience. At the same time it calls his attention to some portion of his experience.

"And you may wonder what that means."

"You'll really know when you have found out."

3. Selectional Restriction Violation

This is the class of surface structures usually referred to as metaphors. They are violations of well-formed meaning as understood by native speakers of a language. When the client hears a sentence with such a selectial restriction violation, the burden of constructing meaning for this communication falls upon him.

"The man drank the rock."

"The flower was angry."

4. Deletion

When a portion of the meaning of a sentence (the deep structure) has no representation of the surface structure (the actual sentence spoken to the client). This leaves the client the freedom to generate the meaning that is most relevant to his experience.

"It seems like an impossible task." (Seems impossible to whom?)

"You're doing the same thing that you did when you first went to school." (Did what? Same as what for whom?)

5. Sentence Fragment

Fragments are pieces of sentences . Such fragments—the result of ungrammatical deletion—force maximum participation by the client to make a complete meaning.

"Take you a while . . ."

". . . and continue to wonder . . . and really . . ."

6. Nominalization

Nominalization is the process of turning a process word or verb into an event or thing. This almost always occurs with the total deletion of some referential index. It forces the client to recover the deleted portions by activating, from his own model of the world the meaning that will best serve his purpose and needs.

"The utter comfort of knowledge and clarity.."

"The presence of relaxation and curiosity . . ."

D. AMBIGUITY

Ambiguity occurs when a surface structure can have more than one meaning. This forces the client to select the most appropriate meaning from the set of possible deep structures that the single surface structure represents.

Ther are four types of ambiguity:

1. Phonological

This kind of ambiguity occurs when the same sound sequence has different meanings.

"The depth was a part and apart."

2. Syntactic

Syntactic ambiguities occur when the syntactic function of a word cannot be determined from the immediate context.

"They are visiting relatives."

"Hypnotizing hypnotists can be tricky."

3. Scope

Scope ambiguity occurs when it cannot be determined from an inspection of the immediate linguistic context how much is applied to that sentence by some other portion of that sentence.

"Speaking to you as a child."

"You will realize that you are sitting comfortably, and you are going into a deep trance."

4. Punctuation

Punctuation ambiguity occurs when a sequence of words results from an overlap of two well-formed surface structures sharing a word or phrase.

"I want you to notice your hand me the glass."

"I notice that you are wearing a watch carefully what I am doing."

E. LESSER INCLUDED STRUCTURE

Surface structures that include another structure can be valuable for giving embedded commands and for building response potential.

1. Embedded questions

Embedded questions build a client's response potential by raising questions without allowing an overt response from the client .They often presuppose some other command.

"I hope that you feel better."

"I wonder whether you know which hand will rise first."

2. Embedded commands

Embedded commands convey suggestions to the client indirectly and thereby make it difficult to resist. They constitute a pattern of surface structures that include a command within them. Similar to embedded questions.

"I knew a man once who really understood how to feel good about . . ."

"You can learn anything if you only give yourself a chance to relax."

3. Quotes

The verbatim presentation of some conversation or verbal exchange, is consciously understood by the listener to be directed at someone in the story, however it often has the effect as through the command had been delivered to the listener directly, except that the listener responds unconsciously.

"Somebody once told me, shut your eyes now."

"What does it mean when someone says, don't move or don't talk?"

F. DERIVED MEANINGS

In using language we assume the listener's ability to hear our surface structures and decode them from sound sequences into meaning. We also assume certain additional abilities to make extra meaning out of what we offer; for example, to establish a context in which what we say could have pragmatic value.

1. Presuppositions

A presupposition is a sentence that must be true for some other sentence to make sense. Since a presupposition is not part of a sentence's deep structure, its use both involves the client as an active participant in making meaning (in this case derived meaning) and puts beyond challenge whatever the presupposition is.

"I wonder whether you are aware that you are deeply in trance?" Presupposition: You are deeply in trance.

"Sam didn't notice the cat on the table." Presupposition: There was a cat on the table.

2. Conversational Postulates

As with a presupposition, the meaning conveyed by a conversational postulate is derived—it is not part of the deep structure recovered by the client but requires additional processing. By using conversational postulates the hypnotist can avoid giving commands simultaneously, thus allowing the client to choose whether to respond and avoiding an authoritarian relationship with the client.

"Can you allow your hand to rise?"

"There is no need for you to move."

References

American Psychiatric Association. *Diagnostic and Statistical Manual of Mental Disorders, Third Edition*. Washington: APA, 1980

Bandler, R. & Grinder, J. *Frogs Into Prices*. Box F, Moab, UT: Real People Press, 1979.

Bandler, R. & Grinder, J. *Reframing: Neuro-Linguistic Programming and the Transformation of Meaning*. Box F, Moab, UT: Real People Press, 1982

Dilts, R., Grinder J., Bandler, R., Bandler, L. & DeLozier, J. *Neuro-Linguistic Programming: Volume I: The Study of the Structure of Subjective Experiences*. P. O. Box 565, Cupertino, CA: Meta Publications, 1980.

Fairbank, J., Langley, K., Jarvie, G. & Keane, T. A Selected Bibliography on Post-traumatic Stress Disorders in Vietnam Veterans, *Professional Psychology*, 1981; 12:578-586.

Grinder, J. & Bandler, R. *TRANCE-formations: Neuro-Linguistic Programming and the Structure of Hypnosis*. Box F, Moab, UT: Real People Press, 1981.

Johnson, W. *People in Quandaries*. New York, NY: harper and Row, 1946.

Korzybski, A. *Science and Sanity: An Introduction to Non-Aristotelian Systms and General Semantics* (4th Edition). Lakeview, CT: The International Non-Aristotelian Library Publishing Co., 1958.

Lankton, S. *Practical Magic: A Translation of Basic Neuro-Linguistic Programming Into Clinical Psychotherapy*. P. O. Box 565, Cupertino, CA Meta Publications, 1980.

Wolpe, J. *The Practice of Behavior Therapy*. Elmsford, NY: Pergamon Press, Inc., 1969.

The Society of
Neuro-Linguistic Programming™

Established in 1978, the Society of Neuro-Linguistic Programming™ is a worldwide organization set up for the purpose of exerting quality control over those training programs and services claiming to represent the model of Neuro-Linguistic Programming™ (NLP). The seal above indicates Society Certification and is usually advertised by Society approved institutes and centers. We highly recommend that you exercise caution as you apply the techniques and skills of NLP. We also urge you to attend only those seminars, workshops and training programs that been officially designed and certified by The Society of Neuro-Linguistic Programming™. Any training programs that have been approved and endorsed by The Society of Neuro-Linguistic Programming™ will display a copy of the registered certification mark(s) of the Society of Neuro-Linguistic Programming™. The Society of Neuro-Linguistic Programming™ is set up for the purpose of exerting quality control over those training programs, services and materials claiming to represent the model of Neuro-Linguistic Programming™.

As a protection for you and for those around you, The Society of NLP™ requires participants to sign licensing agreements which guarantees that those certified and licensed in this technology will use it with the highest integrity. It is also a way to insure that all the trainings you attend are of the highest quality and that your trainers are updated and current with the constant evolution of the field of Neuro-Linguistic Programming™ and Design Human Engineering™.

There are four levels of certification and licensing granted by The Society of Neuro-Linguistic Programming™: Practitioner, Master Practitioner, Trainer and Master Trainer. All certificates issued by The Society of Neuro-Linguistic Programming™, the Society seal, and Richard Bandler's signature in penned ink. Trainers may train Practitioners and Master Practitioners who then may get certified and licensed by Richard Bandler and The Society of Neuro-Linguistic Programming™. Master Trainer is a level recognized because of special circumstances and contributions. This level is reserved and can only be granted by Richard Bandler and The Society of Neuro-Linguistic Programming™. Master Trainers may not certify Trainers except under special written permission of Dr. Bandler.

Design Human Engineering™ (DHE) may only be trained by Trainers of DHE. This level of certification is granted only by Richard Bandler and The Society of Neuro-Linguistic Programming™. Their certificate will specifically state "Trainer of Design Human Engineering™" with the Society Seal and Richard Bandler's signature.

To be sure you are purchasing Pure NLP products and/or services, please call the Society of Neuro-Linguistic Programming™. We are most interested in protecting the technology's integrity. All certifications and licensing carry a two (2) year expiration date, the Society Seal, and Richard Bandler's signature. You have the right to ask anyone advertising NLP services to show you their license and/or certification. An inability to produce this document may one of two possibilities: either the person and/or organization is defrauding the public, or they have been defrauded themselves by another organization purporting to be a certifying organization. Under either condition, please notify The Society of Neuro-Linguistic Programming™ so that we may take steps to rectify the situation.

Each license and/or certification has a two year expiration date. This is because the technology is constantly evolving and Dr. Bandler is continuing his development contributions to human evolution. The Society expects that those who hold certification continually update their skills and renew their certifications and/or licenses. Renewal is not automatic and is easy. Do not accept certifications and/or licenses without expiration dates. If you have benefited from Richard's contributions in the form of the technologies he has developed, we appreciate it when you help us to point out the charlatans who are out there misinforming the public. This is more of a moral issue than anything else. Richard and the Society are interested in people doing the right things and becoming very prosperous in all areas of their lives. There is an unlimited amount of opportunity for everyone. There is no need to steal.

If you are certified at any level of Design Human Engineering™, you must obtain express written permission for each usage of the term or symbol (DHE™) from Richard Bandler. This can be obtained by contacting the First Institute of NLP™ and DHE™ at (415) 955-0541 or 44 Montgomery St., 5th floor, San Francisco, Ca. 94104. Each use of the term Design Human Engineering™ must be earmarked with a (™) as well as a symbol that refers to the phrase "Design Human Engineering™ and DHE™ is used with express written permission of Richard Bandler."

ONLY RICHARD BANDLER, PERSONALLY, MAY TRAIN TRAINERS OF NLP™, except under express written permission from Richard Bandler.

Should you be a member of the Society of Neuro-Linguistic Programming™ and have not complied with the above requirements, we wish to make you aware that you may grandfather your trainees for a limited time.

The Society publishes its directory of members in good standing and is happy to provide referrals upon request and encourages participation in this opportunity to make a difference for everyone.